SOKA GAKKAI IN AMERICA

SOKA GAKKAI IN AMERICA

Accommodation and Conversion

Phillip E. Hammond

and

David W. Machacek

OXFORD

UNIVERSITY PRESS

OXFORD

UNIVERSITY PRESS

Great Clarendon Street, Oxford OX2 6DP

Oxford University Press is a department of the University of Oxford
It furthers the University's objective of excellence in research, scholarship,
and education by publishing worldwide in

Oxford New York

Athens Auckland Bangkok Bogotá Buenos Aires Calcutta
Cape Town Chennai Dar es Salaam Delhi Florence Hong Kong Istanbul
Karachi Kuala Lumpur Madrid Melbourne Mexico City Mumbai
Nairobi Paris São Paulo Singapore Taipei Tokyo Toronto Warsaw

with associated companies in Berlin Ibadan

Oxford is a registered trade mark of Oxford University Press
in the UK and in certain other countries

Published in the United States
by Oxford University Press Inc., New York

British Library Cataloguing in Publication Data

Data available

Library of Congress Cataloging in Publication Data

Hammond, Philip E.
Soka Gakkai in America: accommodation and conversion / Phillip E.
Hammond and David W. Machacek.
Includes bibliographical references.
1. Soka Gakkai—United States—History. 2. Soka Gakkai
International–USA—History. I. Machacek, David W. II. Title.
BQ8412.9.U5H36 1998 294.3'928'0973—dc21 98-32054

ISBN 0-19-829389-5

1 3 5 7 9 10 8 6 4 2

Typeset by Hope Services (Abingdon) Ltd.
Printed in Great Britain
on acid-free paper by
Biddles Ltd.,
Guildford & King's Lynn

4029864

Dedicated to Ninian Smart and the memory
of Walter Capps—splendid colleagues to one of us;
exceptional teachers of the other

Preface

TUCKED away inconspicuously in a business park behind a grove of lemon trees in Goleta, California, stands the Santa Barbara Soka Gakkai community center. The building resembles several other offices surrounding it. The single sign identifying it as belonging to Soka Gakkai International USA (SGI-USA) looks like the signs of the neighbouring businesses. From the outside, one would hardly know that this is a place of religious worship—indeed, a place where about one hundred young, middle-class Southern Californians gather weekly to chant their devotion to a mandala inscribed by a thirteenth-century Japanese monk named Nichiren, and to the Buddhist principles it represents.

Crossing the threshold between the mundane world of daily life and this sacred space of Soka Gakkai Buddhism, we are greeted by attractive and exceptionally friendly people. They seem as excited as we are about the research we are undertaking, and eager to answer any questions we might have. The sound of people chanting in the next room fills the reception area—a constant, soothing, polyphonic hum. We are invited to observe the ritual, and our hostess offers a booklet containing an English transliteration of the Japanese words, so we can "follow along." It takes only a moment to realize that following along is going to be an impossible task for someone unaccustomed to the Japanese language. Instead, we read the English summaries that explain the meanings of the prayers and then relax into the comfortable stoicism of the sociological observer.

There is much to observe. Striking is the eclectic blend of the modern and the traditional. Just left of the altar where the Gohonzon (meaning "object of devotion," the name of the mandala inscribed by Nichiren) is enshrined, stands a television and VCR on a rollaway cart. A man with dark skin kneels on the floor before the altar, leading the prayers of an ethnically diverse group seated on folding chairs. Several of them clasp prayer beads devotionally in front of their face, punctuating the chant by rubbing the beads between the palms of their hands.

It is tempting to read all kinds of meanings into these observations, but we have avoided doing so in this book. As outsiders to the group, we were able to see things from a perspective different from that of insiders, but in no way can we claim to understand the meaning better than the members themselves. Therefore, we allowed the members of SGI-USA to speak for themselves as much as possible, basing our understanding on their statements in SGI-USA publications, in our survey, in follow-up interviews, and in casual conversations.

At the same time, as sociologists, we were not simply documenting what we observed. Although much of the first part of this book is necessarily descriptive, our analytic purpose was to answer certain theoretical questions: (1) How do religions respond to a new social environment? And (2) What makes a new religion appealing to people in that environment?

A series of fortunate events led to our SGI visit and, ultimately, this book. Responding to the study of Soka Gakkai members in Great Britain, published by Bryan Wilson and Karel Dobbelaere in 1994, Virginia Straus, the executive director of the Boston Research Center for the Twenty-First Century—a group funded by Soka Gakkai—recognized the need for accurate data on SGI members in the United States. Through Bryan Wilson, Phillip Hammond was invited to submit a proposal to survey SGI-USA members for this purpose. In addition to providing funds for a survey that would yield the desired statistics descriptive of SGI-USA members, the Boston Research Center allowed Hammond the right to include questions of theoretical interest and to publish the results as he wished. Seeing the opportunity for a graduate student enamored of empirical data, Hammond hired David Machacek as a research assistant. This book is truly a product of their scholarly cooperation.

As is usually the case with a project such as this, there are too many people who deserve credit to mention them all by name. Don Brodale spent many hours reviewing what had already been written about Soka Gakkai, and we relied heavily on his work to familiarize ourselves with the religion. When the time came to mail the surveys, Sara Karesh, Bernie Smith, Ellen Posman, and Julie Ingersoll assisted with the thankless task of stuffing, labeling, and stamping envelopes. Sara Karesh's assistance coding data from the returned surveys made the process not only more efficient but also more entertaining. Later, when the time came to conduct some follow-up interviews with respondents to the survey, Kerry Mitchell joined the team, speaking with SGI-USA members by phone and then transcribing the interviews. The assistance of these people made our task easier, though of course any errors or misinterpretations can be charged to us.

Contents

Introduction

A CONSIDERABLE body of research is now available on new religious movements in the United States. Those religions with roots in Eastern traditions, in particular, captured the attention both of the American public and of academics who study religion in America. Theories of religious conversion and explanations of the seemingly sudden advent of Eastern religions in the United States abound.[1] These circumstances necessitate some justification for offering yet another.

Earlier research examined the characteristics of converts to explain the appeal of Eastern religious traditions among Americans. Often, these studies found converts to the new religions to be somewhat marginal, if not explicitly alienated, citizens of urban America. Former participants in the counter-culture of the 1960s, for instance, found in Eastern religion an alternative to psychedelic drugs as a means of consciousness raising.[2] Participation in an exotic religion offered a way to remain countercultural, but one that was more acceptable than drug use. Thus, for some people who had ventured to the margins, the new religions became a means of re-entry into mainstream social life.

---

[1] See Thomas Robbins, *Cults, Converts and Charisma* (London: Sage, 1988) for a thorough review of this literature.

[2] Steven Tipton, *Getting Saved from the Sixties* (Berkeley: University of California Press, 1982).

1

Other studies posited a more explicit religious seeking for alternatives to mainstream American religion.[3] Urbanization, increasing levels of social and geographic mobility, rising levels of education, changes in family life, and the emergence of a new class of information workers made for social experiences to which the more established religions sometimes failed to give meaning. While some analysts with this perspective lamented the fragmentation of American religious culture, others perceived the beginnings of a process of cultural revitalization. Perhaps the new religions gave meaning to the experiences of a generation coming of age at a time of rapid social change. The new religions, argued Jacob Needleman for instance, provided practical guidance for contemporary life where secular psychology, philosophy, and modernist theologies failed.[4] These studies, and a multitude of others, highlighted social changes that, in turn, led to a *demand* in the American public for religious alternatives.

Recently, however, a growing awareness has emerged among sociologists of religion that, in addition to a changing demand, the past few decades have been characterized by a growing *supply* of religious alternatives. Drawing on the language of market economics, such scholars as Rodney Stark, Roger Finke, and Laurence Iannaccone have demonstrated that the emergence of these alternative religions coincided with a further step in what they called the "deregulation" of the religious market.[5]

In particular, these authors point to the year 1965, when President Johnson rescinded the Oriental Exclusion Act of

[3] Wade Clark Roof, *A Generation of Seekers: The Spiritual Journeys of the Baby Boom Generation* (San Francisco: Harper San Francisco, 1993).

[4] Jacob Needleman, *The New Religions* (Garden City, NY: Doubleday, 1970).

[5] Roger Finke and Rodney Stark, *The Churching of America, 1776–1990: Winners and Losers in our Religious Economy* (New Brunswick, NJ: Rutgers University Press, 1992); Roger Finke and Laurence Iannaccone, "Supply-Side Explanations for Religious Change," *Annals of the American Academy of Political and Social Science*, 527 (1993), 27–39; Laurence Iannaccone, "The Consequences of Religious Market Structure," *Rationality and Society*, 3 (1991), 156–77.

1924, an act passed at a time of religious nativism. Already struggling to cope with the arrival of large numbers of Roman Catholic and Jewish immigrants, to say nothing of the boggling variety of ethnic traditions each encompassed, Protestant Americans were hardly prepared for an influx of people whose religions stood entirely outside of the European, "Judeo-Christian" heritage. Intentional or not, the Oriental Exclusion Act severely curtailed the supply of Eastern religions in the United States.

The years following 1965 thus saw a dramatic increase in the number of Asian immigrants, who brought with them a number of new religious alternatives. Not all of these religions entered the "religious market" as competitive players, of course. Most took the more traditional path of immigrant religions, serving their existing members as a refuge of ethnic identity in the new environment. Some, however, began actively seeking converts, either immediately from the time of their arrival in America, or, as in the case of the group studied here (Soka Gakkai International, or SGI), only after a period of organization and accommodation to the American scene.

While none of these groups ever succeeded in recruiting a large enough number of formerly Protestant, Catholic, or Jewish Americans to pose a real threat to American mainstream religion, they were visible enough to stimulate yet another period of nativist reaction. Many of these groups stood in direct opposition to mainstream culture, encouraging members to reject such sacred American cultural traditions as individualism, capitalism, and even, in some cases, the family. Exotic beliefs and practices such as requiring members to wear distinctive styles of dress, live communally, eat a vegetarian diet, or evangelize in public places were distinctively at odds with the mainstream culture and drew more attention to these religions than their actual size warranted. No wonder it was difficult for parents, siblings, and friends to understand the sudden changes that accompanied conversion to one of these new religious alternatives. Nor is it surprising that, in their opposition to

American culture, these groups would be perceived by many as a threat.

One of the more successful of the new religions, however, managed to grow quietly, largely (though not entirely) avoiding notice during the cult scare, and thereby largely evading the machinations of the anti-cult movement. While such contentious new religions as ISKCON (Hare Krishna) and the Unification Church (Moonies) experienced rapid rise and then sudden decline, the Soka Gakkai grew rather steadily on the sideline. Although the Soka Gakkai's growth rate leveled off and then declined in recent years, it nonetheless achieved organizational stability. Its story is one of low-key perseverance. The enduring success of the Soka Gakkai in America calls for some explanation, and that is the purpose of this study. It is a study of both accommodation and conversion.

Data and Methods

During the spring and summer of 1997, we conducted a survey of Soka Gakkai members in the United States. Self-administered questionnaires were sent to members whose names were drawn randomly from the cumulative list of subscribers to the four main SGI publications distributed in the United States. The questionnaire was thorough, containing 102 questions on many topics: how respondents were introduced to Soka Gakkai and became members, the extent of their involvement, and an extensive series of questions covering their values and attitudes about a number of social issues. We reproduced questions from the survey of SGI members in Great Britain and questions from the General Social Survey conducted annually by the National Opinion Research Center at the University of Chicago. Therefore, we are able to make comparisons between members of the Soka Gakkai in the United States and Great Britain and, more importantly, comparisons between the SGI-USA members and the American public. In all, we received 401 completed questionnaires, which constitute our primary source of information.[6]

Another source of information was personal discussion, chiefly with leaders in the SGI-USA headquarters, but also with SGI members in the Santa Barbara area. These discussions were helpful when we found puzzling results. For example, the number of subscribers to the *World Tribune*, SGI-USA's weekly newspaper, plummeted from over 100,000 during the late 1980s to fewer than 48,000 in 1990. Through a conversation with a national leader, we learned that during the 1980s, SGI-USA encouraged members to buy multiple subscriptions in order to bring financial resources into the organization and for members to use in spreading information about SGI among friends and family. In the late 1980s, this policy was rescinded, and, of course, subscription rates declined. (Membership rates are discussed in Chapter 3.)

A third source of information was telephone interviews conducted in the early months of 1998. We conducted follow-up interviews with (1) members who indicated on their questionnaire that they are highly and enthusiastically involved in SGI, (2) members who indicated on their questionnaire that, though they are still members of SGI, they might drop out someday, and (3) former members whose names were included in our sample but who informed us they are no longer involved in SGI. We had, at the end of the survey instrument, asked respondents if they would be willing to be interviewed by telephone, and, if so, to provide their telephone number and a time they could best be reached. A surprising 63 percent gave us this information.

A final source of information was the scholarly literature on SGI already published. Books include studies of this Buddhist sect in Japan, Great Britain, Canada, and the United States. Many journal articles were also available. Some of these publications contain quantitative data. Most notably, the British

[6] For more information about the survey and the representativeness of our sample, see Apps. A and B.

study, like ours, contained data based on a randomly selected sample. Wherever possible, data from these two surveys are compared to determine whether similar processes are at work in both countries. Much of the information in the other publications is qualitative but provided helpful background information, particularly on the history of the Soka Gakkai in the United States.

Plan of the Book

Apart from what was necessary to complete the story of Soka Gakkai in the United States, we have deliberately avoided making this a study merely of conversion. As we shall see, joining the Soka Gakkai does not seem to entail a radical transformation of world-view. For most of the "converts" in our sample, the basic elements of what we will be calling a "transmodern" view seem to have been in place prior to encountering SGI. An equally interesting conversion story to be told is that of the transformation of a Japanese religious sect into an American religion. More radical change is to be found in SGI itself than in the formerly Protestant, Catholic, and Jewish Americans who have joined SGI over the past forty years. Indeed, the willingness to accommodate itself to the American social environment helps to account for the success of SGI in the United States. Hence our subtitle: "Accommodation and Conversion."

Our primary interest in this study is to develop an understanding of the conditions under which religions appear in a new environment, as well as the processes influencing their performance in that environment. To arrive at such an understanding, it is necessary to consider qualities of the social environment outside of the religions themselves and therefore largely beyond their control. Regulation of religion by the state, public satisfaction with existing religious forms, and widespread cultural assumptions about religious matters are examples of such contexts. These conditions alone, however, do not determine the destiny of an organization.

It is necessary also to consider qualities of the organization itself; actions taken by participants in an organization will influence its performance. Some of these actions are internal to the organization—what happens when a charismatic leader dies, for example—while others are external actions taken in relationship to the social environment.

As we shall see, Soka Gakkai in the United States has been very careful with its "American" image. Here, SGI has emphasized legitimacy, even at the expense of growth. This story, along with a description of Soka Gakkai's philosophy, is detailed in Chapter 1.

Chapter 2 describes the demographic profile of SGI members in the United States. Supporting claims made by the Soka Gakkai, our survey shows SGI-USA members to be racially diverse. They are also drawn from a very respectable, upwardly mobile segment of the US population. Only minor differences are found between the characteristics of members in the United States and Great Britain.

Often there is notable discrepancy between the beliefs and practices as prescribed by a religious organization and the way these prescriptions are actually followed by members. Chapter 3 demonstrates that most respondents to the 1997 survey are faithful to the demands of SGI, in the sense that most are quite—some exceedingly—active in the organization. An index is constructed that classifies respondents according to degree of involvement, and core members are found to differ systematically from marginal members in interesting ways. Chapter 3 is also the place where most of the members' own testimony—taken in telephone interviews—appears.

The three chapters making up Part I are largely descriptive, serving to acquaint the reader with Soka Gakkai and its members in the United States. The three chapters of Part II are more analytical, attempting to develop a coherent story explaining the overall success of Soka Gakkai in the United States. Chapter 4 describes how changes in the American social environment made it possible for new religious movements, including Soka

Gakkai, to compete in this society. Contrary to what would be expected using only the lens of free-market economics, however, those new religions that entered the field *aggressively* sparked controversy, making it more difficult for them to recruit new members and retain the recruits they did gain. Soka Gakkai, by contrast, benefited from a soft-sell, unassertive approach to growth. It assimilated many aspects of American culture, including expectations of how religious organizations should behave. The long-term result has been a degree of organizational stability that most of the new religions never achieved.

In fact, for most of the converts, the transition into Soka Gakkai appears to have been relatively smooth; SGI-USA required little change in their behavior and outlook. Indeed, we have reason to believe that they held, prior to encountering the religion, many of the basic elements of the worldview promoted by Soka Gakkai. This "transmodern" cultural orientation is described in detail in Chapter 5 and related to social changes taking place in post-World War II America.

We examine in Chapter 6 how the organization supplying the religion and the people who are most likely to desire it come together in the process of encounter, recruitment, and conversion. Not every encounter leads to a potential recruit nor every recruitment to a successful convert. We go on, therefore, to ask why some people who are successfully recruited eventually convert, while others drop out and move on to other things. We argue that the determining factor is consistency between the recruits' values and those promoted by Soka Gakkai.

Even those readers already familiar with the Soka Gakkai should learn something new from this study. SGI-USA members will be interested to learn that while we locate their religion at the boundary of religious culture in America, it is the boundary looking ahead to the future, not back to the past. Put another way, SGI is close enough to the cultural center to be a reasonable alternative to the mainstream American religions but distinctive enough to make a singular contribution to the

American religious market. Readers for whom this book is a first introduction to Soka Gakkai Buddhism will encounter a religion that, while less well known in America than, say, Zen, promises to be a lasting presence in the United States. Finally, our most querulous audience—the academic community—will find what we hope is a fresh perspective on the new religions in the United States. Our interpretation of the data has drawn upon classical ideas (notably, Weber's Protestant Ethic thesis), as well as more contemporary debates, particularly the one between proponents of supply-side and demand-side theory.

I

SGI-USA
The Organization and Its Members

1

Soka Gakkai History and Philosophy

SOKA Gakkai International (SGI) is among the less familiar of the new religions in the United States. Other religions of Asian origin, such as ISKCON (Hare Krishna), the Unification Church (Moonies), Transcendental Meditation (TM), and the Divine Light Mission, that emerged in the United States mid-century received more attention (albeit often negative) by both the media and academics. Even readers who are aware of the growing presence of Buddhism in America are probably more familiar with Zen and Tibetan Buddhism because of the large number of popular books written about them and Hollywood portrayals of the Dalai Lama. When *Time* mentioned SGI in its October 20 1997 cover story "Buddhism in America," it was merely to report that Tina Turner practiced it. These circumstances demand, therefore, that we begin with a brief description of Soka Gakkai Buddhism.

History

Soka Gakkai is a twentieth-century lay movement that follows the teachings of a thirteenth-century Buddhist monk Nichiren Daishonin. Nichiren taught a form of Buddhism that differs from most other forms in its this-worldly orientation. Its goal, as understood by the Soka Gakkai, is to help individuals achieve enlightenment and happiness in the present world, and by so doing to create a harmonious society. The ascetic nature of Nichiren Buddhism, or the impulse to reform social conditions in light of religious convictions, is the driving force behind Soka Gakkai's activities. That reforming impulse, however, has made Soka Gakkai controversial, bringing the group into conflict with public authorities in Japan more than once in its seventy-year history.

Although Nichiren Buddhism dates to the thirteenth century, Soka Gakkai is very much a product of modernity. The organization was founded in 1930 by a Japanese educator, Tsunesaburo Makiguchi (1871–1944), as a movement to reform the educational system in Japan. During the Meiji period (1868–1912), education had been used as an extension of government to promote loyalty to the emperor and a sense of national identity. By contrast, influenced by Western ideals, Makiguchi's educational philosophy was more humanistic, oriented to individual achievement and happiness. Whereas the dominant educational philosophy emphasized obedience and rote memorization, Makiguchi encouraged critical thought oriented to personal goals and interests. Furthermore, Makiguchi was critical of objective truth as the goal of education. He believed that students should be taught to pursue value, benefit, or gain, and that they should be encouraged to make a positive contribution to society—thus, the title of his book on education *The System of Value-Creating Pedagogy*.

At first, the Soka Kyoiku Gakkai, or "Value-Creation Education Society," appealed primarily to other, like-minded educators. Although the society grew to several thousand members in the years prior to the beginning of the Pacific War, it never resulted in the educational reforms Makiguchi desired. Instead, Makiguchi's open criticism of the World War II government captured the attention of authorities and earned him a reputation as a political dissident, but far from backing down, Makiguchi broadened the scope of his thinking.

Just prior to the founding of the Soka Kyoiku Gakkai, Makiguchi, along with his disciple Josei Toda (1900–58), converted to Nichiren Shoshu Buddhism—the first step toward making Soka Gakkai a lay organization of this Buddhist sect. Like Makiguchi, Nichiren had been critical of the Japanese government and was subject to persecution for his efforts to reform Japanese society in light of Buddhist wisdom. Makiguchi found in Nichiren's idea of reforming society through individual enlightenment a religious belief that resonated with his ideas about education. As did Makiguchi, Nichiren interpreted the political troubles Japan was experiencing during his day as a result of the propagation of false religious doctrines. Like others in the Tendai sect, an offshoot of the Mahayana school of Buddhism imported from China, Nichiren believed himself to be living in the age of *mappo*. *Mappo*, or "the latter day of the law," was believed to be a time when misunderstandings of the Buddha's wisdom and the promulgation of false doctrines would cause general social malaise.

Nichiren had ample evidence to support his beliefs. During his time, Japan was plagued with earthquakes, fires, disease, and invasion. He believed that a new teacher would come to clarify the Buddha's teachings and make them accessible to the people. As individuals became enlightened through Buddhism, the consciousness of the people would be raised, resulting in an end to crime, war, and poverty in Japan. After years of studying the writings of the Buddha, Nichiren had found the key in the second and sixteenth chapters of the *Lotus Sutra*. He interpreted these writings to mean that all individuals have within themselves the potential for enlightenment, or "Buddhahood." As individuals became aware of their own Buddha nature, they could help others on the path to enlightenment. To facilitate the process of enlightenment, Nichiren prescribed a simple mantra, *Nam-myoho-renge-kyo*, which translates, "devotion to the mystic law of the *Lotus Sutra*," and inscribed a mandala, known as the Gohonzon, or "object of worship," which expresses this rule of faith. The Gohonzon is understood as a mirror of the individual's inner Buddha nature. By chanting *Nam-myoho-renge-kyo* in front of the

Gohonzon, the individual attempts to realize that Buddha nature.

Because of his conviction that other sects were teaching dangerous and false doctrines, and his insistence in petitions to the government that his own form of Buddhism be preferred, the government persecuted Nichiren. Narrowly escaping execution, Nichiren spent much of his later years in exile. Following his death, Nichiren's followers broke into several sects. Nichiren Shoshu, or "the orthodox sect of Nichiren," claims the most direct lineage from Nichiren, through the sect's first high priest, Nikko, down to the present head priest, Nikken. Although it never became the official religion of Japan, Nichiren Shoshu eventually achieved a stable position among the smaller sects of Buddhism in Japan.

This comfortable existence began to change, however, as Japan's militant government prepared for war, in part by extending its control over religion through the Religious Organizations Act (1940). This act consolidated religion into thirteen sects of Shinto, twenty-eight sects of Buddhism, and two sects of Christianity. This three-religion establishment existed under a canopy of State Shinto, which "was created by the government and nationalistic Shinto theologians after the Meiji restoration in order to . . . legitimize the newly built government and to unite the people under its authority."[1] Shinto thus became the official cult of the state, and the state required citizens to observe ceremonial events as a means of enhancing nationalism.[2]

The anti-authoritarian Makiguchi objected to the use of religion to promote nationalism, just as he had objected to the use of education for this purpose. When ordered to enshrine a Shinto talisman as a sign of national loyalty, Makiguchi and his followers refused. Consequently, he and several of his followers were arrested and imprisoned as enemies of the state. Most of his followers ultimately capitulated and were subsequently

[1] Tsuyoshi Nakano, "New Religions and Politics in Post-War Japan," *Sociologica*, 14/12 (1990), 4–5.
[2] Ibid. 5.

released. Makiguchi, however, and his disciple Toda were resolute and remained in prison for the duration of the war. Makiguchi died in prison in 1944, leaving Toda to rebuild the organization after the war.

In prison, Toda grew increasingly committed to Nichiren Shoshu. He claimed to have achieved enlightenment during his incarceration after chanting *Nam-myoho-renge-kyo* (also referred to as *daimoku*) over 2 million times. Whereas Makiguchi had emphasized study and education, Toda focused on practice and devotion. After he was released from prison following the war, Toda reorganized the Soka Gakkai, dropping the word Kyoiku ("education") from the name. Thus an organization that began with an emphasis on educational reform became one devoted to promoting devotion to the *Lotus Sutra* and the teachings of Nichiren.

Toda's zealotry earned him a mixed reputation in the Japanese public and gave Soka Gakkai a controversial public image. Under his leadership, Soka Gakkai developed a reputation of intolerance for other religions and was suspected of having despotic aspirations. The practice of aggressive recruitment, known as *shakubuku* (which has been translated "break and subdue"), and the practice of smashing household ancestral altars by zealous new members did little to improve the group's image in the public eye. Massive rallies and parades held by Soka Gakkai at the time reminded onlookers of similar demonstrations by the fascist regimes of World War II. Thus, an organization whose founder was persecuted for his opposition to militant nationalism and the use of religion to bolster political sovereignty came to be suspected by many of harboring aspirations for a theocratic government. Accusations of despotic intent and militant nationalism have haunted Soka Gakkai throughout its seventy-year history. Nonetheless, Toda's success as a leader is unquestionable. By the time of his death in 1958, the Soka Gakkai had grown to over 750,000 members.[3]

[3] The reputation of being "intolerant" has plagued Nichiren Shoshu Buddhism throughout its history, more during some periods than others. See

Soka Gakkai continued to grow under Toda's successor, Daisaku Ikeda. Under Ikeda's leadership, the group's radicalism has been toned down, although it maintains a distinctively anti-authoritarian and reformist stance with regard to the political and religious establishment. As a means of recruitment, Soka Gakkai has stopped the practice of aggressive *shakubuku*, opting instead for a more low-pressure, "show by example" approach, known as *shoju*. Furthermore, Soka Gakkai has diversified its involvement in Japanese society, founding a university, art museums, a concert association, a publishing empire, and elementary and secondary Soka schools based on the educational theory of Makiguchi. In 1964, Soka Gakkai established a political party, called Komeito, or the "clean government party," dedicated to promoting world peace through globalism, egalitarianism, and democratic government.[4] Although protesting freedom of religion is one of the main points of Komeito's platform, Komeito immediately drew suspicion as a "religious" party. After a couple of decades and limited success in parliamentary politics, Komeito dissolved, becoming part of a coalition of opposition groups, the New Frontier Party, in 1995.[5] Soka Gakkai's current political activity consists of endorsing individual candidates and partisan groups depending on the issues. Today, with over 8 million members, it is the largest sect of Buddhism in Japan. Moreover, since 1960, it has developed affiliate organizations to promote Nichiren Buddhism worldwide, and now claims members in North and South America, Europe, and other Asian countries. In 1975, Soka Gakkai International (SGI) was formed, with headquarters in Tokyo, to link together the organizations found in nations around the world.

Despite such achievements, Soka Gakkai remains controversial in Japan — in large part, because of its anti-authoritarian,

Jacqueline Stone, "Rebuking the Enemies of the Lotus: Nichirenist Exclusivism in Historical Perspective," *Japanese Journal of Religious Studies*, 21/2–3 (1994), 231–59.

[4] Nakano, "New Religions and Politics in Post-War Japan", 17.

[5] "Soka Gakkai's Relations with the Komei Party," *Soka Gakkai News* (Sept. 1994), 20.

reformist stance. Ironically, much of the criticism has been directed at Soka Gakkai's third president, Daisaku Ikeda, who has not held executive powers in the organization for nearly twenty years. Ikeda is a charismatic figure who inspires considerable loyalty among Soka Gakkai members, and he has been active in meeting with world leaders to discuss his vision of world peace. It is not difficult to perceive why Soka Gakkai has been described as "Ikeda worship." In the administrative offices of the Soka Gakkai and SGI in Tokyo, as well as in the buildings of affiliated organizations, one finds pictures not of the Soka Gakkai's current president, Einosuke Akiya, but of Ikeda. And in discussions on virtually any topic with Soka Gakkai members in Japan, President Ikeda's opinions are sure to be mentioned. Despite the fact that, in 1979, Ikeda stepped down as president of the Soka Gakkai, maintaining only his title as an honorary president, and a symbolic role as an inspirational leader, public suspicion remains about him.

Although members of Japan's dominant Liberal Democratic Party have portrayed Soka Gakkai's involvement in politics as a threat to freedom of religion in Japan, it is probably as a reform movement, rather than as a religious movement, that Soka Gakkai poses its greatest threat to the establishment. Komeito was officially separated from the Soka Gakkai in 1970 as a response to criticisms of the political party's ties to a religious sect, but Soka Gakkai members continued to support a Komeito-style agenda. Soka Gakkai's political efforts have been rather successful overall, and with over 8 million members, it represents a sizeable voting block. For this reason, the Liberal Democratic Party, which represents the business establishment and unions, has taken measures to restrict Soka Gakkai's political activities. So far, these measures have been unsuccessful. That the political establishment would use the banner of religious freedom to legitimate efforts to restrict Soka Gakkai is yet another irony of the situation of Soka Gakkai in Japan.

Of course, the self-image of Soka Gakkai is quite the opposite of that held by many in the Japanese public. Soka Gakkai members perceive themselves as a people's movement dedicated to creating a good society based on Buddhist principles—a Japanese equivalent, in some respects, to the Christian Coalition in America. Although vocal in its support of religious freedom and its opposition to government intervention in religious affairs, the Soka Gakkai's this-worldly asceticism—its commitment to the creation of a good society, and thus its concern for social reform—drives Soka Gakkai into the arena of political activity, thus making it difficult to shed rumors of ulterior motives.

The anti-authoritarian stance of the Soka Gakkai also led to the excommunication of Soka Gakkai by the Nichiren Shoshu priesthood in 1991. Despite the history of political activism by Nichiren himself, the Nichiren Shoshu priesthood has traditionally taken a more conciliatory stance toward Japanese society. The priesthood is built on the patriarchal model of organization characterizing much of Japanese society. Because of its populist direction, Soka Gakkai experienced tensions with the priesthood periodically throughout its history. Those tensions became more acute during the 1970s. Ikeda's personal charisma and popularity among Soka Gakkai members caused the priesthood to consider him a threat to their authority. It was at their behest that President Ikeda stepped down as the leader of Soka Gakkai in 1979. This move allayed tension for a time, although Ikeda continued to inspire the dedication of Soka Gakkai members as the symbolic leader of the movement.

A crisis developed in 1989, however, when the priesthood decided to raise the fees for obligatory priestly services at weddings and funerals. Soka Gakkai leaders objected and were accused of being disrespectful of the priests. In statements regarding the relationship of lay members to the priests, made early in 1990, Ikeda asserted that the teachings of Nichiren were more authoritative than those of the priests. The priests, in turn, argued that such criticism of the priesthood was a slander against Buddhism, and ordered Soka Gakkai to submit an explanation and apology. Soka Gakkai, in response, asked for dialogue with the priesthood about the issue, which the priest-hood refused, demanding again a written apology. This time, SGI challenged the priesthood's actions as authoritarian and undemocratic, accusing the priests of making unilateral de-cisions about the Soka Gakkai without consulting its members. As the conflict grew, both sides closed ranks. In November 1991, the priesthood issued a notification of excommunication of the Soka Gakkai and all of its members. Excommunication meant barring access to official transcriptions of the Gohonzon, prohibiting pilgrimages to the temple, and denying funeral and marriage services to Soka Gakkai members.[6]

The 1991 schism has been compared to the Protestant Reformation, and rightly so.[7] The parallels are striking. The priesthood has hurled accusations of heresy at the Soka Gakkai, claiming authority based on a lineage of priests going back to Nichiren's chosen disciple Nikko. The Soka Gakkai, in reply, asserts that devotion to the *Lotus Sutra* as explained in Nichiren's writings, not devotion to the priesthood and the traditions it represents, is all that is necessary for enlightenment. They have asserted the priesthood of believers, appointing "ministers of ceremony" to conduct—without a fee—marriage and funeral services,[8] and playing down the significance of pilgrimage to Taiseki-ji, the head temple where the Dai-Gohonzon, inscribed by Nichiren himself, is enshrined. The Soka Gakkai has begun issuing the Gohonzon reproduced from one transcribed by Nichikon—the predecessor of the current high priest, Nikken. Most striking is the parallel between SGI's accusation of money-hungry priests selling *toba*—memorial

[6] These moves are ironic, to say the least, since the fees paid by laity to the priests for such services are a major source of the priesthood's revenue. Jane Hurst, "A Buddhist Reformation in the Twentieth Century: Causes and Implications of the Conflict between Soka Gakkai and the Nichiren Shoshu Priesthood," Paper presented at the Harvard Buddhist Studies Forum Conference, Harvard University, Cambridge, Mass., May 1997.

[7] Ibid.; Daniel Metraux, "The Dispute between the Soka Gakkai and the Nichiren Shoshu Priesthood: A Lay Revolution against a Conservative Clergy," *Japanese Journal of Religious Studies*, 19/4 (1992), 325–36.

[8] At the present time, these ministers are temporary volunteers.

tablets offered on behalf of the dead—for personal gain and the Protestant Reformation's objection to priests selling indulgences.

Although couched in terms of doctrinal legitimacy, the dispute between the Nichiren Shoshu priests and the Soka Gakkai is best understood with reference to the very different identities of the two organizations. Nichiren Shoshu is a product of feudal Japanese culture—an era when values of duty, loyalty, obedience, and tradition reigned. The priesthood, laying claim to the authority of tradition and the charisma of office, is thus more church-like in orientation. Having achieved a degree of establishment status with deep and abiding roots in Japanese culture, the priests have been willing to make concessions to the surrounding society, and have taken a compliant stance with regard to the political establishment. Thus, as we saw, the priests complied with the requirement to enshrine a Shinto talisman in 1943, becoming a part of the three-religion establishment in support of State Shinto, while Makiguchi and Toda went to prison rather than compromise their faith—an event the Soka Gakkai have not forgotten.

Soka Gakkai, on the other hand, is a product of modernity—an age when science, reason, and technology displace the authority of tradition. Born in the tumultuous time when an authoritarian government led Japan into a disastrous war, and raised on the democratic ideals of the Occupation Government, Soka Gakkai has been characteristically suspicious of power and authority, usually adopting an anti-establishment position, in both politics and religion. While the priests assert the authority of tradition, Soka Gakkai is an organization dedicated to reform. The authority of Soka Gakkai's leaders is based not on office or lineage, but, instead, on charisma, talent, and consent of the followers. Where the priesthood is more church-like, Soka Gakkai is thus more sect-like.

It was probably only a matter of time, therefore, before the reforming and anti-authoritarian stance of the Soka Gakkai would lead to conflict with the traditional and conservative priesthood. It is hardly surprising that the younger and more energetic Soka Gakkai would feel restrained by the seasoned formalism of the priesthood. It was certainly only a matter of time before the priesthood would come to perceive the relatively autonomous, reform-oriented Soka Gakkai as a threat to its authority. Under Ikeda's leadership, the Soka Gakkai had been turning its attention toward its own program, developing its own institutions, and turning away from its earlier emphasis on recruiting human and economic resources for the priesthood. Given this trend and Ikeda's popularity with Soka Gakkai members, it is not difficult to understand why the priesthood would perceive a challenge to its well-being. It is also understandable that the priesthood's attempt to assert authority over the anti-authoritarian Soka Gakkai would stimulate rebellion.

Since 1991, relations between the Soka Gakkai and the Nichiren Shoshu priests have continued to be strained. SGI has used its publishing empire to publicize its side of the conflict and to raise questions about the priesthood's legitimacy. The priests, in turn, have attempted to win over the laity, offering access to the temple and priestly services in exchange for renouncing the Gakkai and swearing allegiance to the priests. Such retributive actions as the demolition in 1997 of the Grand Reception Hall built by the Soka Gakkai within the Taiseki-ji compound are indicative of the bitterness of the dispute. On April 8 1998, the priesthood announced plans to demolish as well the Grand Main Sanctuary, Sho Hondo, which has housed the Dai-Gohonzon since the building was completed in 1972, mainly with funds collected by the Soka Gakkai. At this time, reconciliation does not appear likely.

Soka Gakkai in the United States

An observer of the Soka Gakkai in the United States could hardly guess that the religion's history in Japan is one of controversy and schism. Apart from a minor and short-lived controversy concerning the development of a branch of Soka

University in Los Angeles, the movement in the United States was barely noticed during the cult scare of the 1970s and 1980s. In part this is because, by the time the American anti-cult movement got organized, Soka Gakkai had already stopped sponsoring high-profile events, such as parades and mass rallies. Members of the movement looked and acted like the public at large, so that, unless one had a friend who belonged, or happened to be approached by someone still doing *shakubuku* on the street—a practice that was officially ended in the mid-1970s—one would hardly know that the religion existed at all. Most who came into contact with the religion did so privately, and that contact increasingly turned toward a soft-sell, "try it and see" approach. In the United States, there developed a small group of disgruntled ex-members, who have been the primary source of whatever "anti-cult" sentiment has been directed at SGI-USA, chiefly through an occasional mimeographed newsletter. We can assume charges made against SGI-USA were largely ignored, however. As we shall see later, while over half of our respondents report negative reactions to their joining Soka Gakkai, these tensions apparently dissipated quickly. In fact, most of those who encountered the movement and decided not to pursue it simply left quietly. Compared to other new religions that entered the American religious market at about the same time, then, the history of Soka Gakkai has been rather tranquil.

Soka Gakkai first arrived in the United States in the mid-1950s with the Japanese wives of American military men. The absence of Nichiren Shoshu temples, combined with the organization's patriarchal structure and the relatively small and scattered number of members, made for a quiet history during the religion's first fifteen years in the United States. In 1960, however, the newly elected President Ikeda set his sights for the expansion of the movement overseas, focusing particularly on the United States and Europe. Shortly after his election, Ikeda visited the Soka Gakkai members living in the United States, encouraging them to organize for the spread of Soka Gakkai within the country. Appointed to lead the organization in the United States was Masayasu Sadanaga, a Japanese immigrant who arrived in America in 1957. Sadanaga set the stage for Ikeda's visit and established headquarters for the movement in Santa Monica, California. By changing his name to George Williams in 1972 (chosen because of the frequency of those first and last names in the Los Angeles telephone book), he set the trend of Americanization that would characterize the movement in the United States.[9] For example, Williams's own book on SGI-USA (entitled *Freedom and Influence: The Role of Religion in American Society*) begins with a lengthy analysis of church-and-state relations and the history of religion in America.[10]

At first, recruitment efforts in the United States targeted other Japanese immigrants. Members would look for Japanese names in the phone book and attempt to make contact with them.[11] No doubt, for those new members recruited in this way, Soka Gakkai offered an opportunity to socialize with other Japanese immigrants and to maintain a sense of connection with their cultural heritage. These early meetings were conducted in the traditional manner; participants spoke Japanese, removed their shoes at the door, and knelt on the floor to chant *daimoku* before the Gohonzon.

By 1963, however, sufficient numbers of English-speaking members warranted holding discussion meetings in English. Shortly thereafter, recruitment of non-Japanese members began in earnest. At first, in addition to inviting family and friends, members would be sent into public places, where they would approach strangers and attempt to bring them back to a

[9] Hideo Hashimoto and William McPherson, "Rise and Decline of Sokagakkai, Japan and the United States," *Review of Religious Research*, 17/2 (1976), 82–92.

[10] George M. Williams, *Freedom and Influence: The Role of Religion in American Society (An NSA Perspective)* (Santa Monica, Calif.: World Tribune Press, 1985).

[11] David Snow, Shakubuku*: A Study of the Nichiren Shoshu Buddhist Movement in America, 1960–75* (New York: Garland, 1993), 100.

discussion meeting. However, the Soka Gakkai watched and learned from other new religions in the United States.[12] As these other groups drew nativist fire from the American public, Soka Gakkai ceased the practice of making cold contacts in public places, relying instead on the warm contacts that could be made through family and friends. By the end of the 1970s, Soka Gakkai in the United States had shifted its recruitment goals, emphasizing the quality of the converts' personal growth through involvement, not the quantity of new recruits.[13] Rather than draw negative attention through zealous proselytizing, the Soka Gakkai hoped to attract new members by demonstrating the positive transformations taking place in the lives of those currently practicing.

The Soka Gakkai has been very careful with its "karma" in the United States, making adjustments as necessary to avoid scandal, presenting a positive image, and accommodating American members, while maintaining the fundamental message of human revolution through devotion to the *Lotus Sutra*. Citing the doctrine of *zui ho bini*, which states that Buddhism can be "taught according to the particular characteristics of a certain society," so long as the essential teachings are not compromised, the Soka Gakkai assert that Nichiren Buddhism is not bound to Japanese culture and society.[14] It can and should be taught using the resources available in the surrounding culture. It is, according to SGI, destined to be a global religion and should be accessible to all who would be citizens of a peaceful and harmonious world.

From the late 1980s and in the 1990s, the Soka Gakkai's primary growth strategy has been one of positive public relations. Indeed, it would seem that SGI-USA has shifted its emphasis from recruitment to establishing itself as a valid and

---

[12] Daniel Metraux, *The History and Theology of Soka Gakkai: A Japanese New Religion* (Lewiston, NY: Edwin Mellen, 1988), 107–8.

[13] Jane Hurst, "The Nichiren Shoshu Sokagakkai in America: The Ethos of a New Religious Movement", Ph.D. thesis, Temple University, 1980.

[14] *NSA Quarterly* (Summer 1976), 146.

desirable religious alternative in America. Attention has been significantly refocused away from the complex national organization and toward the local group, whose members are encouraged to be active in the community.

In addition, the Soka Gakkai in the United States has been receptive to inquiry by scholars. Indeed, the Soka Gakkai has been receptive to criticisms raised in earlier studies of the movement. Rather than react defensively, the Soka Gakkai treated such criticisms as valid and made adjustments in the organization's practices. For instance, a criticism of the patriarchal nature of the SGI-USA leadership stimulated the Soka Gakkai to open national leadership roles to women. Similarly, SGI-USA has been criticized for the undemocratic polity of its leadership.[15] Already in 1980 the organization was shifting its focus from the national leadership toward autonomous local groups. By 1997 the structure of the national leadership had been greatly reformed—from an executive director assisted by various appointed officials to a legislative body representing the major territories in the United States.

Soka Gakkai Belief and Practice

The heart of Soka Gakkai Buddhism is the goal of world peace through individual enlightenment. To this end, Soka Gakkai maintains three pillars of faith—chanting, study, and *kosen-rufu* (the spread of Buddhism in the world).

Chanting

By chanting *daimoku* (*Nam-myoho-renge-kyo*) and *gongyo*, which consists of portions of the *Lotus Sutra* and prayers for world peace, the Gakkai members believe they can change their karma. Karma, as understood by Soka Gakkai Buddhists, is "the cumulative effect of the causal forces produced by everything

---

15 Hurst, "Nichiren Shoshu Sokagakkai in America", 221.

one thinks, says, and does."[16] Karma should not be misunderstood as fate or destiny. There is an element of fatalism in the Gakkai notion of karma in that one's current experience results from actions in past lives. However, to Soka Gakkai Buddhists karma is more like the Western idea of character or momentum. That is, one's experience of life is not the result of conditions in the individual's environment so much as the attitudes, or "causes," one brings into that environment. There is a strong emphasis in Soka Gakkai on the individual's personal responsibility for his or her circumstances in life. By chanting, individuals attempt to take control of their way of being in the world, and thereby overcome obstacles and accomplish specific goals.

President Ikeda, an avid reader who often takes inspiration from the classics, writes of an episode in the life of Leo Tolstoy that illustrates this idea of karma very well. The episode involves one of Tolstoy's sons, Ilya, when he was a young boy:

One day, the boy was given a cup and saucer that he had wanted for a long time. Overjoyed, he wished to show it to everyone. He rushed around the house almost beside himself with excitement. But between one room and the next there was a high doorsill. Ilya tripped over it; the cup went flying and was smashed to pieces.

The boy broke into loud sobs. When his mother scolded him, telling him that it was his fault for being careless, he got angry and tearfully retorted: "It's not my fault. It's the builder's fault! Why did he put a doorsill there?" Tolstoy, who overheard, roared with laughter. He never forgot these words.

From then on, whenever members of his family tried to justify themselves by blaming their mistakes on others, Tolstoy would grin and ask, "It's the builder's fault, right?"[17]

While members may joke about chanting to win the lottery or buy a new Cadillac, chanting is not understood as a magic

[16] Robert Eppsteiner, *The Soka Gakkai International: Religious Roots, Early History and Contemporary Development* (Cambridge, Mass.: Soka Gakkai International—USA, 1997).

[17] Daisaku Ikeda, "Take Responsibility for your Life," Speech to the 1st Okinawa Executive Conference, Onnason, Japan, Feb. 23 1997; repr. in *World Tribune* (Apr. 18 1997), 9, 11.

formula whereby one can manipulate the external world to serve one's own purposes. In our telephone interviews with members, this point is made frequently, suggesting that members are sensitive to the *appearance* of practicing magic. Rather, chanting is a means by which the individual comes to understand his or her own contribution to the circumstances causing unhappiness. The Soka Gakkai see obstacles as challenges to be overcome. One member in Arizona explained how chanting works this way: "you're putting the will out. Once it's out there, it goes into place . . . There's a freedom of choice. Most of the responsibility is placed on the individual." One's external circumstances, in other words, are an effect of the causes one makes (one's karma). It is believed that by changing one's karma, or rather consciously making a cause for a particular goal, one can effect a change in external circumstances.

Thus, the effect of changing karma is a transformation of one's "life condition." According to the Soka Gakkai, every individual has the potential for ten states of life, known as the "ten realms." These ten realms range from the lowest—Hell, Hunger, Animality, and Belligerence—through the intermediate realms—Humanity, Heaven, Learning, and Realization—to the highest—Bodhisattva and Buddhahood, or Enlightenment. According to Soka Gakkai teachings, everyone "possesses and intermittently experiences each of these life states."[18] However, these states are not merely moods, but "patterns into which one's entire existence falls."[19] The goal of Soka Gakkai Buddhism is to establish and maintain a state of enlightenment, which is achieved when people break their dependence on external circumstances for finding satisfaction and begin to take responsibility for their own state of being in the world.

Soka Gakkai asserts that members will experience improvement in their external circumstances as this process occurs. These external benefits are seen as "proof" that chanting works. However, to repeat, chanting is not magic. When Soka Gakkai

[18] Eppsteiner, *Soka Gakkai International*, 9. [19] Ibid.

members chant for a new car, better relationships, or such, the goal is to effect internal changes that allow them to take control of their external circumstances and achieve these goals.

This rather individualistic orientation is couched in the collective goal of world peace. The Soka Gakkai believe that as individuals become enlightened and improve their own life conditions, the lives of people around them will also be improved. Thus, potentially, the conditions of life for everyone can be raised, resulting in general prosperity and ultimately world peace.

Finally, there is a mystical element in chanting. The Gohonzon inscribed by Nichiren—which features the *daimoku* written down the center surrounded by various Buddhas, Boddhisatvas, and gods representing the ten realms—is held to be a mirror of the individual's inner Buddha self and an expression of ultimate reality. The truth of Nichiren Buddhism is both subjective, residing in individuals and their experience of the world, and objective, the universal law portrayed in the Gohonzon. Chanting the *daimoku* forms a bridge of sound and vibration between the individual and the Gohonzon, such that subject and object become one. Thus, some Soka Gakkai members report mystical experiences during chanting. One Soka Gakkai member in Santa Barbara, for instance, described an experience while chanting before the Gohonzon in which the "words seemed to come off the page" toward him.

To the Soka Gakkai Buddhist, the universal, mystical truths of Buddhism are experienced in practical, everyday life. Subject and object, cause and effect, are one. Chanting, foremost, raises people's awareness of their state of consciousness and way of being in the world. Second, chanting raises awareness of the impact of this subjective life condition on external circumstances and on the lives of others. And ultimately, chanting raises people's awareness of their connection with the universe and the ultimate laws that govern it.

Study

Study is not so much the study of Buddhism as it is the study of the Buddhist approach to life. To Soka Gakkai Buddhists, study means learning to interpret life experiences through the lens of Buddhism as taught by Nichiren. It is thus understood broadly in Soka Gakkai to include both a growing knowledge of Buddhist doctrine and the pursuit of better living through art and the humanities. The materials offered for study, such as the *World Tribune* (a weekly newspaper) and *Living Buddhism* (a monthly glossy), draw inspiration as often from non-Buddhist authors as from the writings of Nichiren or the *Lotus Sutra*. As mentioned already, President Ikeda is an avid reader who refers frequently in speeches and writing to material he's been reading. In so doing, he models the pursuit of wisdom by relating humanistic studies to Buddhist doctrine.

Soka Gakkai sponsors numerous cultural activities, such as art exhibitions, festivals celebrating the diversity of the world's cultures, marching bands, and dance troupes. They have built institutions of higher education, museums, a concert association, research institutes, and retreat centers. Such activities are not merely peripheral adjuncts to the religion. As the lotus flower is to the muck at the bottom of a pond, so are art and culture to Soka Gakkai Buddhists living in the age of *mappo*. Through art and culture, Soka Gakkai cultivates a happier, more peaceful and harmonious reality than that which now exists in the modern world.

Kosen-rufu

Kosen-rufu refers to the spread of Nichiren Buddhism in the world. Soka Gakkai members believe that only by raising consciousness of their inner Buddha-nature can individuals become happy, and chanting devotion to the *Lotus Sutra* is the best way to achieve this goal. As Nichiren Buddhism spreads, more and more people will achieve happiness, and this will result in a peaceful world. While the primary goal of world peace has remained constant, the Soka Gakkai's understanding of how *kosen-rufu* is to be achieved has changed dramatically over time.

Earlier in the religion's history, the Soka Gakkai believed world peace would be achieved only after a critical mass of the world's population had converted to Nichiren Shoshu Buddhism. This understanding was the driving force behind the Soka Gakkai's earlier, more aggressive recruitment techniques and intolerance toward other religions. Elements of this earlier exclusiveness remain, but today the trend is toward an understanding that a small portion of the population, working individually and collectively to make positive causes in their environment, can effect change in the lives of many. Consonant with this change in Soka Gakkai outlook, there is less emphasis now on rapid growth than there was in the past. As observed already, Soka Gakkai has mostly abandoned the aggressive practice of *shakubuku* as a means of recruitment, adopting instead the more passive, "show by example" recruitment method of *shoju*.

Increasingly, Soka Gakkai members are coming to understand themselves as people with a special role to play in world history. While recruitment efforts are being scaled down, more emphasis is being placed on the development of affiliated organizations, such as Soka University, cultural and educational programs, research institutes, and the like. In so doing, Soka Gakkai is "fuzzying the boundaries," as it were, and making it possible for non-Buddhists to join in the cause of world peace without first becoming Soka Gakkai members.

In many ways, Soka Gakkai exhibits a kind of activist millennialism. Members and leaders look to the twenty-first century with optimism as an era when world peace will be realized through international cross-cultural dialogue and the abolition of weapons of mass destruction. Unlike many forms of millennialism, however, the Soka Gakkai do not look for external changes or the intervention of some external deity to effect this transformation. Rather, they understand that external changes will result from internal changes in individuals. Peace, according to Soka Gakkai Buddhists, begins with individual peace and happiness, and spreads as enlightened individuals become active in the cause of peace at the local, national, and international levels. SGI members chant for world peace, but their efforts do not end there. The organization, for example, is also a non-governmental organization member of the United Nations.

Organization

Soka Gakkai International is a complex international organization. The headquarters in Tokyo serves primarily as a communication center where the many national chapters can contact one another to share information, and from which leaders can distribute information around the world. Each of the national chapters is autonomous, organized independently to oversee activities within each nation where Soka Gakkai exists.

SGI-USA is one of the largest of the Soka Gakkai chapters outside of Japan. With its national headquarters in Santa Monica, SGI-USA is subdivided into joint territories (now called regions), divided according to concentrations of SGI members throughout the United States. Within each region, the organization is further subdivided into territories (now called areas), headquarters (now dropped as an organizational level), chapters, districts, and finally, small neighborhood groups consisting of five to ten members. SGI is further organized into divisions defined by age, gender, and specific functions, such as the Culture Department or Student Division or public relations.

Needless to say, such a complex organization requires a considerable amount of labor. With the exception of national, full-time staff, volunteers provide most of this labor. Leadership can involve a great deal of traveling and other expenses, and most leaders are expected to cover their own expenses. The selection of leaders is based, therefore, on a combination of recognized commitment to SGI and ability. While earlier in the religion's history in the USA, leaders were appointed by higher-ranking officials, today the process is one of nomination, review, and approval that involves both peers and leaders.

Perhaps the most notable quality of SGI's organization is its bureaucratic form. The organization has moved increasingly toward the form of a rational bureaucracy, in which leaders execute specific functions and are selected on the basis of specific skills, and away from the earlier, more traditional form in which movement into leadership was based on personal, master–disciple relationships.

Still, there are many opportunities to assume leadership positions in Soka Gakkai. About 70 percent of the currently active members have held or now hold leadership positions at the group level, 55 percent of them leadership positions at the district level, 31 percent at the chapter level, 20 percent at the headquarters level, and about 10 percent at the area and national levels. Members are also often involved in planning, organizing, and participating in such activities as culture festivals and peace committees. In short, SGI-USA is a very busy organization.

In Conclusion

Soka Gakkai's millennialism, anti-establishment position, and this-worldly orientation distinguish it from other sects of Buddhism. In Japan, the movement grew rapidly in the period following World War II, an expression both of dissatisfaction with traditional forms of Japanese social order and of hope for the new democratic and capitalist system that was developed in the period of occupation. Although earlier analyses of the Soka Gakkai in Japan pointed out the possibility of its developing into a totalitarian movement of the sort associated with feelings of alienation in mass society,[20] the organization does not seem to have gone in that direction. That potential remains, of

[20] James White, *The Soka Gakkai and Mass Society* (Stanford, Calif.: Stanford University Press, 1970).

course, and suspicion about the aims of the movement will probably persist in Japan, certainly as long as President Ikeda remains the focus of attention, and maybe beyond because of SGI's commitment to change in *this* world.

In the United States, characteristics of a mass movement are largely absent. As we shall see, in America the Value Creation Society seems to appeal primarily to those who stand to benefit most from the economic and social changes taking place as the twentieth century comes to a close.

The Membership
of SGI-USA

T HE membership of Soka Gakkai has undergone considerable change during its nearly four decades in
America. In this chapter, we present a demographic
profile of the membership based on the 1997 survey, comparing
this profile with earlier reports on the religion as well as with
data on Soka Gakkai in Great Britain. Together they tell a dramatic story of the changing face of Soka Gakkai in the United
States. At the time of its foundation, the membership of SGI-
USA was almost exclusively Japanese. Today, Japanese members are in the minority. In both the United States and Great
Britain, SGI is overwhelmingly composed of new-class Baby
Boomers.

It should be kept in mind that some differences between our
data and the two other sources of information on Soka Gakkai
might be caused by differences in method. Earlier studies of the
Soka Gakkai in America relied upon official rolls or other
sources such as SGI publications. Social scientists are acutely
aware of reliability problems in such sources. No standard exists
among religious organizations for keeping data on membership. Who is and is not included as a member, the frequency
with which membership rolls are cleaned of non-active members, and accuracy in keeping records vary widely from one
religious organization to the next. Furthermore, religious
organizations, particularly those working to carve out a place in

a new environment, have a vested interest in inflating membership rolls. An organization such as the Soka Gakkai has a further vested interest in demonstrating its appeal to mainstream Americans.

Social scientists often differ as well in the methods used for gathering data, depending largely on the interests, methodological training, and budget of the researchers, and the accessibility of the group being studied. Head counts, for example, will usually give results that differ from those obtained in a random sample. However, for many groups, including new religions whose suspicion of a researcher's intentions may inhibit cooperation, head counts may be the only means of data collection. Researchers who conduct interviews as a means of gathering qualitative data commonly report the demographic characteristics of the people interviewed, but such data often fall short of statistical validity. They may tell more about the kind of people who were willing to speak with an interviewer than they do about the group as a whole. Random sampling is generally accepted as the best means of gathering accurate data, short of a population census, and this was the method adopted for this study.

Membership

As recently as 1997, SGI-USA claimed to have over 300,000 members in the United States.[1] Our best information on membership, however, suggests that this number is greatly inflated. New religions are prone to high rates of attrition, and Soka Gakkai is no exception. Typical of the pattern of religious experimentation associated with new religions, many no doubt tried the practice for a while before moving on to other experiments. Others may continue to chant privately before their personal copy of the Gohonzon, although they have ceased to participate in organized group activities. In other words, the boundaries separating Soka Gakkai members from non-members are not

[1] Eppsteiner, *Soka Gakkai International*, 15.

hard and fast. In fact, compared to many of the more high-profile new religions, the boundaries encompassing Soka Gakkai are relatively diffuse; it is not difficult for people to drift in and out of the organization. Chances are, the number of members claimed by SGI-USA better reflects the number of people in the United States who have ever received a Gohonzon, whether or not they ultimately remained involved in the organization.

Since SGI-USA keeps no regional, let alone national, membership figures, subscriptions to SGI publications are the best indicators of its active membership. Given the significance of study to the practice, Soka Gakkai members are strongly encouraged to subscribe to one or more of the main SGI publications. Although estimates based on subscription rates will obviously miss some people who can rightly be considered members, and may therefore underestimate the actual size of the membership, subscriptions remain the best source available. Figure 1 shows the subscription rates for the four publications most commonly read by American members, from 1964 to the present.[2] From these data, it is readily apparent that the movement is much smaller than it claims to be.

Obviously, subscriptions to the *World Tribune* do not provide an accurate measure of membership. Figure 1 shows huge peaks and valleys in its subscription rate, which are cause for suspicion. The *World Tribune* is an inexpensive weekly newspaper that has served as a public relations device as well as a source of information about the movement's activities worldwide for SGI members. Stories included in the *World Tribune* cover the achievements of SGI members, particularly those of its president, Daisaku Ikeda. In the past, SGI-USA has sponsored subscription drives, both as a means of recruitment and as a source of revenue for the national headquarters. Indeed, the most recent peak in *World Tribune* subscriptions, during the decade of the 1980s, coincides with a period when the Soka Gakkai

[2] Data provided by Greg Martin, Director, Department of Communication and Planning, SGI-USA Headquarters, Santa Monica, California.

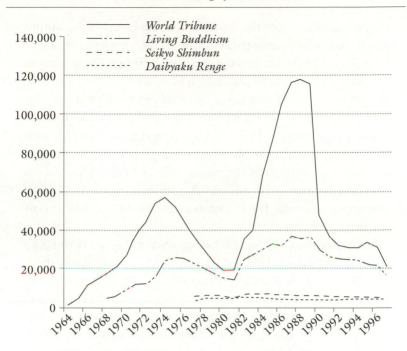

Figure 1. US subscription rates to four SGI publications from 1964

encouraged members to take out several subscriptions to the *World Tribune*, so they would have extra copies to share with persons who might take an interest in learning more about the movement. The sudden decline in subscriptions following 1989 coincides with a change in this policy, as we pointed out in the Preface.

Furthermore, we know from our survey that some of the people receiving the *World Tribune* have never been members of the Soka Gakkai. Well-meaning family members, neighbors, or friends purchased subscriptions as gifts to these people, no doubt hoping they would find inspiration and take an interest in chanting. Also, newcomers who do not continue for long in the religion may have subscribed as a part of their experience but continue to receive the *World Tribune* until their subscriptions expire. In fact, out of the 1,185 names included in the sample list, we know the membership status of 506 people, and 24 percent (N = 122) of them are not active members. This number includes those who responded, telling us that they were no longer members or had never been members, plus those who were unreachable at the address provided. We concluded, in consultation with the SGI-USA headquarters in Santa Monica, that the latter are probably also no longer active in the organization. If 24 percent of the people on the SGI-USA subscription lists are not active SGI-USA members, then the 21,967 subscriptions to the *World Tribune* (as of 1996) represent only 16,695 active members.

Subscriptions to *Living Buddhism* are very likely a better basis for estimating the number of active English-speaking members. *Living Buddhism* is a more expensive, glossy magazine, containing study materials as well as articles about SGI activities throughout the world. It stands to reason that newcomers who are merely experimenting with the practice would be less likely to subscribe to *Living Buddhism*. Therefore, subscriptions to this publication probably provide a more accurate estimate of the number of committed members. This assumption is justified by the fact that the number of active members estimated above, based on subscriptions to the *World Tribune* (16,695), approximates the number of subscriptions to *Living Buddhism* (17,102).

Subscription rates to the two Japanese language publications have been more constant over time and demonstrate less disparity in the number of subscriptions. They are similar in quality and content to the *World Tribune* and *Living Buddhism*. One is a weekly newspaper, *Seikyo Shimbun*; the other, *Daibyaku Renge*, is a magazine. In the United States, however, *Seikyo Shimbun* does not serve the dual function of keeping current members informed and stimulating interest in potential recruits. Therefore, an estimate of the number of Japanese-speaking members can be based on the average rate of subscription for these two publications, which comes to 5,069.

Using the subscription rates to *Living Buddhism* and the average rate of subscription to the two Japanese language publications as a basis, it is possible to estimate the number of *currently active* members of SGI-USA. It can be assumed that each subscription represents a household, since it is unlikely that households containing two or more members would take out more than one subscription. The 1997 survey of SGI-USA members can be used to estimate the average number of SGI members per household. Table 1 provides this information. Thus 26 percent of the respondents have a spouse who is also an SGI-USA member. We can estimate therefore that, on average, each subscription represents approximately 1.26 members when spouses are taken into account. Adding one or more children who are members, we estimate that each subscription represents approximately 1.62 SGI-USA members, which, when multiplied by the current number of subscribers to *Living Buddhism* and the two Japanese language publications (22,171, cumulatively), yields an estimated active membership of 35,917.

This may seem a rather small estimate compared to the 300,000 members claimed by the Soka Gakkai. However, it must be noted that our estimate represents currently active members. It does not capture all the many thousands of people who have been introduced to the practice but no longer pursue

Table 1. Family members who also belong to SGI-USA

Family who are members of SGI	% of SGI-USA members	Factor
Spouse	0.26	0.26
One child	0.11	0.11
Two children	0.07	0.14
Three children	0.02	0.06
Four children	0.01	0.05
Sum		1.62

Note: Questions 17 and 18 in the questionnaire, App. C.

it, or the many who continue to chant privately but are no longer affiliated with the organization. Given the investment of time and effort required to learn the *gongyo*, the exotic nature of the Soka Gakkai belief system relative to mainstream American religion, and the rather high rates of attrition in new religions generally, SGI-USA's growth from roughly 4,000 members in 1965 to over 35,000 active members at the end of this century is an impressive achievement. Compare this number, for instance, to the number of active members in two, more highly publicized new religions. In 1993, ISKCON (Hare Krishna) had about 3,000 core members and claimed about 25,000 lay constituents[3]—numbers that may be just as inflated as the Soka Gakkai's claim of 300,000 members. In 1988 the size of the Unification Church's (Moonies) membership was estimated at 5,000 and declining.[4] If we add to these figures the fact that SGI-USA lost some members during the 1991 schism, and the fact that its growth took place during a period when new religions were looked upon with suspicion, then we indeed have a success story.

Transformation from an Immigrant Religion

SGI-USA has gone to some lengths to reformulate its identity from a religion of Japanese immigrants into an American religion. It has done so not only through proactive assimilation of Japanese members as the organization itself adjusted to American culture, but also through competitive recruitment of non-Japanese Americans. By and large, it has been successful in this strategy.

Ethnicity

Estimates of the proportion of Asian members have varied over time and with the method of gathering data. According to

---

[3] J. Gordon Melton, *Encyclopedia of American Religions*, 4th edn. (Detroit: Gale Research Inc., 1993), 921.
[4] Ibid. 754–5.

George Williams, the proportion of Asian members dropped
from 96 percent in 1960 to 30 percent in 1970.[5] Using published testimonials in the *World Tribune*, David Snow found as
few as 4 percent Asian members in the early 1970s, but it stands
to reason that Asian members would be less likely to write
letters to the English language publications.[6] Of the respondents to our 1997 survey, 15 percent are Japanese. However,
tests for representativeness suggest that Japanese members may
be under-represented in the sample.[7]

Once again, subscription rates provide the most accurate
data. In 1997, there were 17,102 subscriptions to *Living
Buddhism*. The average subscription rate for the two Japanese
language publications in 1997 was 5,069. Out of 22,171 total
subscriptions, therefore, approximately 23 percent are subscriptions that belong to Japanese-speaking members. This figure is higher than one might have expected based on trends
reported in earlier research. It is also much higher than the proportion of Japanese members in the United Kingdom (9 percent).[8] It is nonetheless indicative of the fact that SGI-USA is
no longer a religion of immigrants.

The current membership reflects an impressive level of racial
diversity (Table 2). SGI-USA members are more diverse, in fact,
than the American population according to the 1990 Census.
No doubt, the racial diversity of SGI-USA members is partially
a function of the religion's concentration in major urban areas,
but it is also certainly a function of the religion's professed
values; Soka Gakkai strives to reach out to people of all walks of
life and actively celebrates the diversity of its members.

---

[5] George M. Williams, *NSA Seminar Report 1968–71* (Santa Monica, Calif:
World Tribune Press, 1972).

[6] Snow, Shakubuku, 196.

[7] See App. B.

[8] Bryan Wilson and Karel Dobbelaere, *A Time to Chant: The Soka Gakkai
Buddhists in Britain* (Oxford: Clarendon Press, 1994), 41.

Table 2. Racial profile (%)

Race	SGI-USA		1990 US Census
	Entire sample	Converts only	
White	42	51	78
Black	15	18	12
Asian, Pacific Islander	23	11	1
Latino, Hispanic	6	7	9
Other [a]	15	13	0.1
N [b]	384	311	241,716,000

Note: Question 94 in the questionnaire, App. C.

[a] Includes respondents of mixed race.

[b] The number of cases in this table and subsequent table may vary because of missing responses to some questions.

Religious Origins

The membership of SGI-USA today is made up primarily of converts who come from a wide variety of religious backgrounds. Only 10 percent of the respondents were raised in Soka Gakkai, 8 percent in some other form of Buddhism, and 1 percent in Shinto. The remaining 81 percent converted to Soka Gakkai from another religious background (Table 3). Compared to the distribution of denominational affiliation in the American public, we find that the religious backgrounds of SGI-USA members are disproportionately mainstream Protestant, Roman Catholic, and Jewish. Persons raised with no religious affiliation mirror the American public. SGI converts tend not to come out of conservative Protestant backgrounds (compare, for instance the Southern Baptist row of Table 3).

In brief, Soka Gakkai is a religion on the periphery of the American mainstream, composed primarily of persons who converted from the mainstream American religious traditions.

Table 3. Religious background (%)

Religion raised	SGI-USA		GSS
	Entire sample	Converts only	
Protestant:	39	48	61
Baptist	10	12	11
Southern Baptist	1	2	10
Methodist	4	5	10
Lutheran	4	5	5
Missouri Synod Lutheran	—	—	2
Presbyterian	4	5	4
Episcopal	3	4	2
Other	13	16	17
Catholic	27	33	24
Jewish	5	6	2
None	8	10	9
Other:	22	4	4
Soka Gakkai, Nichiren Shoshu	10	—	—
Other Buddhist	9	—	—
Other	3	4	—
N	381	310	11,892

Note: Question 11 in the questionnaire, App. C.
Source: The source for the last column is General Social Survey (GSS), 1988–1996.

Age, Gender, and Marital Status

SGI-USA members are somewhat older than the US population (Table 4). The median age of Soka Gakkai members is 45 years, compared to the median age of 42 for respondents to the General Social Survey. This difference reflects the concentration of Baby Boomers among SGI-USA members. Respondents to our SGI-USA membership survey are 1½ times more likely than the American public to be in the cohort born between 1946 and 1962. They are less likely to be in either the older or younger birth cohorts. The concentration of Baby

Boomers might be accounted for by the timing of SGI's entry into the American religious market were it not for the relatively meager showing of the post-boom cohort. If timing alone were the issue, we would expect members of this younger cohort, popularly referred to as "Generation X," to be represented at least in proportion to their size in the American population. They are not. The post-boom cohort comprises 30 percent of respondents to the 1996 General Social Survey, but only 16 percent of *all* Soka Gakkai members, and only 14 percent of SGI converts. If this pattern holds, SGI-USA members will, in coming years, have a median age even older than at present.

Table 4. Age, gender, and marital status

	SGI-USA		GSS
	Entire sample	Converts only	
Age mean	46	46	45
Age median	45	45	42
Age cohort (%):			
Generation X	16	14	30
Boomer	57	61	37
Preboom	28	26	33
Gender (%):			
Male	32	34	44
Female	68	66	56
Marital status (%):			
Married	41	38	48
Living with a partner	8	8	n.a.
Divorced, separated	19	21	20
Widowed	5	5	10
Single, other	27	28	23
Has been divorced (%)	38	44	24

Notes: Questions 90, 89, 96, and 97 in the questionnaire, App. C.
n.a. = not available to GSS respondents.

Source: The source for the last column is General Social Survey (GSS), 1996.

The age distribution of SGI-USA members is largely accounted for by a known relationship between religious behavior and the life cycle. That is, people are most likely to convert to a new religion when they are young and relatively free of existing social obligations such as careers and families. Referring once again to the subscription rates in Figure 1 as an indicator of the growth pattern of SGI-USA, two major periods of recruitment and growth appear—from 1964 through 1975, and again from 1982 to 1990. The dates when respondents to the 1997 SGI-USA Membership Survey first began chanting reflect this pattern (far right column of Table 5). The oldest members of the Baby Boom cohort would have been graduating from high school and entering college (and therefore entering the period in the life cycle when they were most likely to have the freedom to experiment with religion) at the beginning of the first major period of SGI growth. Note that the proportion of Boomers among new recruits to SGI-USA triples from 22 percent prior to 1964 to 66 percent from 1964 to 1975— the Boomers' early adult years. Growth slows from 1976 to 1981, when the Boomers were most likely to be getting married and entering full-time occupations and therefore less free to move around in the social world.

The second major period of growth, from 1982 to 1990, reflects the time when the younger cohort were just beginning

Table 5. Date when converts first encountered SGI-USA (%)

Date	Generation X	Boom	Pre-Boom	All
Prior to 1964		22	78	3
1964–75	1	66	33	34
1976–81	2	76	24	14
1982–90	25	56	18	39
1991 and later	33	57	10	10
N	41	178	73	292

Note: Question 1 in the questionnaire, App. C.

to enter college, and therefore most likely to be available for recruitment.[9] After 1982, the proportion of new converts who fall into the younger birth cohort is roughly the equivalent of their representation in the US population. It can be concluded, therefore, that the age characteristics of SGI-USA members are partially a function of life cycle patterns in the American public, and it can be expected that, over time, any SGI-USA growth will come increasingly from the Generation X and later birth cohorts.

Even so, the Baby Boomers remain over-represented among the most recent recruits, suggesting that the unique counter-cultural experiences of the Boomer generation are also involved. Indeed, Machacek has shown that Generation X is somewhat more traditional in their religious outlook and behavior in their early adult years than were the Boomers.[10] Where religion and lifestyle are concerned, the Boomer cohort, it seems, was more experimental than those both older and younger, and thus more likely to get involved in an alternative religion. One inference, of course, is that only if another age group comes along experiencing something of what the Baby Boom experienced will SGI-USA once again find candidates especially ripe for recruitment. By no means does this bode disaster, but it does suggest the likelihood of steadier, smaller rates of recruitment.

The countercultural orientation of SGI-USA converts is evidenced by the marital status of members. Compared with the American public, converts to SGI-USA are less likely to be married, though the margin decreases if we add the number who replied that they are currently unmarried but living with a long-term partner (Table 4). The roughly 8 percent of SGI-USA members who indicated that they are currently living with a domestic partner includes both heterosexual couples who have

---

[9] More will be said about availability and recruitment in Ch. 6.

[10] David W. Machacek, "Generation X and Religion: The General Social Survey Data," Paper presented at the Annual Meeting of the Society for the Scientific Study of Religion, Nashville, Tenn., 1996.

not married, and a number of people who volunteered that they are currently in a same-sex relationship. Furthermore, converts to SGI-USA, compared with the American public, are almost twice as likely to indicate that they have been through a divorce (though we have no way of knowing whether the divorce occurred before or after joining SGI-USA).

At the time of its founding, SGI-USA was overwhelmingly composed of Asian women. Today, women remain in the majority by a margin of 2:1. Indeed, when we asked respondents what originally attracted them to SGI, several of the men quipped, "the beautiful women." This fact notwithstanding, religious intermarriage no longer seems to be a primary means of conversion to SGI-USA. Only five percent of the converts in our sample indicated that they were first introduced to SGI by their present or future spouses. Indeed, as we shall see later, marriage and family life is not a priority for many members of SGI-USA.

Political Views

SGI-USA members tend to fall on the liberal end of the political spectrum. They overwhelmingly supported Bill Clinton in the 1996 election. Sixty-nine percent of them said they voted in 1996, and of those, 78 percent voted for Clinton. Compared to 34 percent of the American public, 59 percent of SGI-USA members align themselves with the Democratic Party, while only 11 percent identify themselves as Republican (compared to 28 percent of the American public). When asked to describe their political views on a scale from one to seven—one being the most liberal and seven the most conservative—SGI-USA members locate themselves on the liberal end. While the modal (most frequently chosen) response in both samples is 4—the center of the scale—a larger proportion of SGI-USA members located themselves on the liberal, or "left", end of the scale than did respondents in the 1996 General Social Survey (51 percent vs. 27 percent).

Education and Vocation

Over time, the occupational profile of Soka Gakkai members in the United States has moved increasingly in the direction of the professional and managerial class. Since the founding members were mostly Japanese wives of American military men, it is not surprising that the earliest recruits were often associated with the military. As of 1968, Snow estimates that approximately 41 percent of SGI-USA members were associated with the military through either employment or marriage.[11] By the 1970s, this proportion had dropped to around 9 percent.

Meanwhile, the proportion of members who were identified as full-time students nearly doubled, from 18 percent to 30 percent.[12] In the early 1970s, the proportion of members Snow classified as holding white-collar occupations had risen to nearly 50 percent. These changes foreshadow the later occupational profile of members.

In 1997, the proportion of SGI-USA members who are currently in full-time education has dropped to less than 5 percent (Table 6), with a corresponding increase in the proportion employed in professional, technical, and other white-collar occupations (66 percent). The representation of persons engaged in military service is now minuscule in comparison to earlier reports. Additionally, the proportion of full-time housewives has dropped from about 16 percent in the early 1970s to around 9 percent in 1997.[13]

The concentration of professional and "new class" information workers in the SGI-USA membership is noteworthy. The proportion in professional, managerial, and administrative occupations is much higher than we find in the general public. Correlatively, industrial, blue-collar workers are notably absent. Despite a decrease from the earlier period, SGI members are still more likely than the American public to be currently engaged in full-time education.

---

[11] Snow, Shakubuku, 202. [12] Ibid. [13] Ibid. 199.

Table 6. Occupation profile (%)

Occupation	SGI-USA	GSS, age adjusted
Professional, managerial, administration	40	29
Clerical, sales, technical support	26	22
Blue-collar	6	24
Service	12	11
Military	—	—
Housewives	9	11
Students	5	2
Other	2	—
N	363	2,889

Note: Question 91 in the questionnaire, App. C.

Source: The source for the last column is General Social Survey (GSS), 1996. Adjusted to match the age distribution of SGI-USA.

This over-representation of professional workers might be explained by underlying factors, such as the concentration of Baby Boomers, who entered the labor force at a prosperous time in America when these new-class jobs were becoming available. In the general public, Boomers are more likely than their parents' generation (born before 1930) to have achieved degrees in higher education, and therefore to be eligible for careers requiring technical or specialized knowledge. However, the finding holds for each age group. Nor is this finding attributable to the concentration of Soka Gakkai in urban environments; the finding also holds when the General Social Survey respondents are limited to persons living in urban environments.

Whether the occupations and educational achievements of SGI-USA members indicate upward mobility is impossible to say for certain because we do not have data on their parents. That is, we have no way of knowing whether the parents of SGI-USA members were more or less educated than their children, or where they stand relative to these SGI-USA members in terms of socio-economic status. Still, we suspect upward mobility, because this is true of Boomers generally in the American public. Furthermore, we can conclude with reasonable certainty that the education and occupation profile of SGI-USA members shows them to be in social positions with the greatest *potential* for upward mobility.

Our survey also indicates that women in SGI-USA are more likely than American women generally to be employed in the labor force, especially in full-time occupations (Table 7); less than half of the women in the American public, but two thirds of the women in SGI-USA, are employed full-time. Women in SGI, especially women converts, are much less likely than American women generally to be full-time homemakers.

Table 7. Employment status of women (%)

Status	SGI-USA		GSS, age adjusted
	Entire sample	Converts only	
Employed full-time	64	68	49
Employed part-time	10	9	14
Student	3	2	2
Housewife, not otherwise employed	10	8	19
Retired, pensioned, unemployed	14	13	16
N	261	205	1,619

Note: Question 92 in the questionnaire, App. C.

Source: The source for the last column is General Social Survey (GSS), 1996.

Given these findings, it comes as no surprise that SGI-USA members are educational achievers (Table 8). SGI-USA members are considerably more likely than the American public (66 per cent vs. 33 percent) to have completed at least some college, more likely to hold a baccalaureate degree (40 percent vs. 26 percent), and they are about twice as likely to have an advanced degree (17 percent vs. 9 percent).

Table 8. Highest level of education completed (%)

Education level	SGI-USA		GSS, age adjusted
	Entire sample	Converts only	
Grammar school	4	2	14
High school	30	36	53
Some college	26	19	7
Bachelor's degree	23	24	17
Graduate or professional degree	17	19	9
N	393	321	2,902

Note: Question 102 in the questionnaire, App. C.

Source: The source for the last column is General Social Survey (GSS), 1996.

SGI in the United States and Great Britain

The demographic profile of SGI-USA members is consistent with that of SGI members in the United Kingdom. A few differences, however, are worthy of note.

SGI members in the United States are less likely than their peers in the United Kingdom to be self-employed (23 percent vs. 32 percent, respectively).[14] This reflects the high proportion of SGI members in the United Kingdom who are engaged in the graphic and performing arts. Whereas 24 percent of the SGI members in the United Kingdom name performance or graphic art professions as their primary occupation,[15] only 6 percent of SGI members in the United States are so employed. SGI members in the United States are more likely than their British counterparts to be employed in administrative and office jobs.

These minor differences, however, do not change the overall picture of SGI members in both countries. In both the United States and Great Britain, a strong concentration of SGI members are engaged in the "caring professions," such as social

[14] Wilson and Dobbelaere, *Time to Chant*, 115.   [15] Ibid. 120.

work, health care, beauty care, and education. In both cases, SGI members employed in manual and industrial work are in the minority. The majority of members in both countries are employed in the professional knowledge occupations.

Differences do show up in the age at which SGI members in the two countries completed full-time education. SGI members in Great Britain are more likely than their counterparts in the United States still to be in school, with approximately 6 percent in the United Kingdom still in full-time education,[16] compared to 3 percent in the United States. This finding suggests a somewhat younger average age of members in Great Britain, but in both nations SGI members achieve higher levels of education than is the standard for the surrounding public.

In Conclusion

In both the United States and Great Britain, then, the demographic picture of SGI members is one of a solidly middle-class population. Overwhelmingly, the converts to SGI in both nations are drawn from the Baby Boom cohort, which began entering the labor force, degrees in hand, at a time when highly educated employees were in great demand. SGI members are typically people who benefited most from the economic changes that began taking place in the United States and Great Britain mid-century. Such a striking finding demands further inspection and explanation. We take up that task in the second half of this book. A full understanding of the relationship between the pattern of Soka Gakkai's development in the United States and social changes taking place in twentieth-century America, however, requires first a closer examination of the religion as it is practiced by the members themselves, the topic of the next chapter.

[16] Wilson and Dobbelaere, *Time to Chant*, 122.

3

The Practice of
Soka Gakkai Buddhism

W E have already described how chanting, study, and the goal of world peace through individual enlightenment are three main pillars of Soka Gakkai Buddhism. However, any religion as it is actually practiced and understood by the members themselves can vary considerably from what is officially prescribed. This chapter describes Soka Gakkai Buddhism as it is practiced and understood by the members who responded to the 1997 survey.

We begin by classifying respondents according to their degree of involvement in SGI. Two dimensions of involvement—private and social—are identified and used to categorize respondents as core, general, or marginal members. As might be expected, the respondents' understanding of their religion and their commitment to its practices vary with degree of involvement.

Involvement

Despite successful efforts to Americanize Soka Gakkai in the United States, Soka Gakkai is a religion on the periphery of American mainstream religious culture. Thus we expect to find two contradictory but related social influences on involvement. On the one hand, we expect rather high levels of attrition. Social pressure by family members, co-workers, and friends tend to discourage dramatic transformations of world-view, and this in turn will result in high attrition among recruits to a religion distinctive from the dominant culture. On the other hand, these very pressures also tend to "weed out" those who are merely experimenting or lacking in enthusiasm, leaving as members those who are most committed. Among those who ultimately choose to continue with the new religion, therefore, we expect relatively high levels of involvement. As a general rule, the average level of involvement in a religious organization rises directly with the religion's "uniqueness" relative to the religious mainstream.[1] Members of Soka Gakkai in the United States are no exception to this rule.

In the last chapter, we noted that the actual number of active members is much lower than the official tally. According to those results, up to 90 percent of the people who received Gohonzons in the United States are no longer active in SGI. It should be noted that this attrition estimate is probably high, since the definition of membership used in this study is relatively strict. Nonetheless, attrition from SGI-USA has been high, as would be expected.

No doubt some of that attrition can be traced to the schism between Soka Gakkai and the Nichiren Shoshu priesthood. Some SGI members chose to align themselves with the temple, becoming members of *hokkeko*—lay organizations associated with the temples. However, in the United States, membership in *hokkeko* numbers no more than a few thousand.[2] Most of the attrition is a matter of simply dropping out. We spoke with one such drop-out, whose experience is probably typical: "I just kind of slowly decreased. It wasn't a total stopping point. I just [dropped] off—doing it less and less and going to meetings less and less . . . I think perhaps that if my husband had joined, that would have made a difference for me. But, . . . this didn't click with him and eventually didn't with me either."

---

[1] Laurence Iannaccone, "Why Strict Churches are Strong," *American Journal of Sociology*, 99 (1994), 1180–1211.

[2] Hurst, "A Buddhist Reformation".

Some people who stop attending SGI-USA meetings continue to chant privately, remaining Soka Gakkai Buddhists therefore, though not involved in the religious organization. We spoke to several such people in our follow-up interviews. Two of them indicated that, while they enjoyed chanting and found the practice beneficial, they simply had no interest in organized religion, preferring instead to keep their spirituality private. Thus, one reported that she liked Soka Gakkai and had no negative thought about it, except "a sort of generalized negative thought about anything organized—religious wise." Another described his experience with Soka Gakkai as one stopping-off point in his on-going spiritual journey. For him, "SGI was a good organization . . . to get my feet wet in, to understand, and to associate with people and get their ideas," but he "yearned to grow in different directions"—specifically, to explore other spiritual alternatives, such as ESP, spiritualism, even other varieties of Buddhism.

Indeed, once one has learned to chant, there is no necessary reason to continue participation in organized activities. The practice of Soka Gakkai Buddhism is oriented, foremost, to individual spiritual growth. While many find the support, guidance, and camaraderie of other SGI-USA members helpful, others prefer to chant privately, seeking the companionship of other members only on special occasions, such as weddings or funerals, or when faced with particularly challenging obstacles. By denying the necessity of priestly intervention, and emphasizing the individual's relationship to the Gohonzon, Soka Gakkai established its independence from the priesthood but also removed a primary reason for members to participate in the collective life of the organization. These three factors—uniqueness primarily, but also the schism and the individualistic orientation of Soka Gakkai—result both in high rates of attrition and in a large number of members who are only marginally involved in collective activities.

Among those who are active in the organization, however, involvement is generally high. Of the ten or so indicators of involvement included in the survey, four are the most straight-forward: (1) frequency of chanting, (2) frequency of reading SGI publications, (3) frequency of attending SGI-USA gatherings, and (4) the number of family and friends who are members of SGI.

1. *Chanting.* The prescribed practice requires SGI members to chant the *gongyo* twice every day. Since this takes around forty minutes to complete, chanting requires a considerable investment of time as well as personal discipline. Nonetheless, 62 percent of the SGI members in the sample chant twice daily as prescribed, and 76 percent say they chant at least once a day (Table 9).

Table 9. Frequency of chanting (%)

Frequency of chanting	% of members
Never	2
Less than 7 times a week	22
7-13 times a week	14
Twice every day	62
N	378

Note: Question 24 in the questionnaire, App. C.

2. *Study.* As with chanting, most SGI members surveyed report spending time every week reading SGI publications, which contain both news about SGI activities worldwide and materials for study. Seventy-six percent of the respondents report reading at least two of the four publications on a regular basis. Of course, since the sample was drawn from subscription lists, such a high number is not surprising. Table 10a reports the amount of time SGI members say they spend every week reading each of the four main SGI publications distributed in the United States. On average, SGI-USA members spend about three hours every week reading SGI publications. The discrepancy between the amount of time spent reading the first two

Table 10. Time spent reading SGI literature (%)

(*a*) By all members

Time	World Tribune	Living Buddhism	Seikyo Shimbun	Daibyaku Renge
None	11	24	84	86
1 hour	60	50	7	6
2–3 hours	23	20	5	4
4 or more hours	7	6	5	3
N	386	381	355	352

(*b*) By members born in Japan

Time	Seikyo Shimbun	Daibyaku Renge
None	25	31
1 hour	25	26
2–3 hours	25	24
4 or more hours	25	19
N	60	58

Note: Question 38 in the questionnaire, App. C.

publications and the other two is of course because *Seikyo Shimbun* and *Daibyaku Renge* are Japanese language publications. When the sample is limited to SGI-USA members born in Japan (Table 10*b*), the results are more evenly distributed.

3. *Attendance at SGI gatherings*. While the frequency of chanting and time spent reading SGI literature are skewed toward the high end, the two remaining involvement variables are more discriminating. Still, both the reported attendance at SGI gatherings and reported number of family and friends who are SGI members demonstrate rather high levels of involvement.

As mentioned earlier, once one has learned to chant, there is no necessary reason for participation in SGI-sponsored group activities. Attendance at Soka Gakkai events is encouraged but not required by the practice. It stands to reason, then, that attendance at SGI gatherings, such as the weekly *gongyo* held at local community centers, and participation in cultural festivals or neighborhood groups would be among the more discriminating indicators of involvement. Even so, the majority of SGI members say they spend two hours or more every week at SGI gatherings (Table 11).

Table 11. Weekly attendance at SGI gatherings (%)

Time	% of members
Never	13
1 hour	24
2–3 hours	31
4–10 hours	26
11+ hours	7
N	377

Note: Question 38 in the questionnaire, App. C.

4. *Family and friends in SGI.* Table 12 shows the number of the respondents' family members and friends who are also members of SGI. More than half of the respondents reported having at least one family member who belongs to Soka Gakkai, and 34 percent have two or more. The vast majority said that they have close friends who are Soka Gakkai members. A mere 7 percent of the respondents reported neither friends nor family in the religion.

At face value, these indicators would suggest that most SGI-USA members are highly involved in their religion, with very little variance. The results, shown in raw form, therefore merit further discussion. To the alert reader, such invariability would raise questions about the validity of the sample. In a religion the membership of which is composed primarily of converts, is it

Table 12. Relationships with SGI-USA members (% of members)

No. of family members:	
0	46
1	18
2	16
3	7
4+	11
N	399
No.of friends:	
0	13
1–2	30
3–4	21
5–6	15
7–8	7
9+	14
N	341
No. of family and friends:	
0	7
1–2	23
3–5	32
6–10	25
11+	13
N	340

Note: Questions 17 and 23 in the questionnaire, App. C.

realistic, for instance, to believe that close to half have family who are members of Soka Gakkai? And given the constraints on free time among working Americans, and the competition for that time by family obligations, work, and entertainment, is it realistic to believe that 60 percent of SGI-USA members spend close to an hour every morning and evening chanting?

In regard to the validity of the sample, two considerations should be kept in mind. First, the sample was drawn from subscribers to SGI-USA publications. The very act of buying a subscription to a religious publication suggests a certain degree of involvement. As already noted, the sample consists almost exclusively of currently active members. Those who remain affiliated with SGI-USA, but are not currently active, those who are in the process of dropping out, and former members who have already dropped out are under-represented in the sample. Second, as noted earlier in this chapter, there are good reasons to expect members of a religion on the periphery of American mainstream religious culture to exhibit relatively high levels of involvement. The number of family and friends in SGI is not surprising either. As will be discussed in Chapter 6, it is often through these kinds of social ties that people are introduced to Soka Gakkai in the first place. And it stands to reason that persons who did not develop friendships or other interpersonal ties to other members would be less likely to remain involved in the religion. With such considerations in mind, then, high rates of involvement might be expected.

Nonetheless, the question remains as to whether these indicators can be used to measure *degrees* of involvement among currently active members. Statistically all four of these variables hold together so strongly that they merit collective treatment as indicators of an underlying hypothetical variable that describes involvement.[3] However, simply adding the four variables together would result in an index that is too heavily skewed toward the high end to be of any real use in discriminating degrees of involvement. Logic suggests a more effective way to handle these variables.

Chanting and study differ from the other two indicators in that they can be performed privately without any contact whatsoever with other SGI members. As demonstrated above, these

---

[3] Spearman correlations range between 0.184 and 0.460. All are significant at $p < 0.000$. A principal-components analysis reveals a single-factor solution that explains 47.2% of the variance in the hypothetical variable.

two variables also represent the most common ways of being involved in Soka Gakkai. Almost all of the respondents to the survey chant regularly and spend time reading SGI materials. The second set of variables, having family and friends who are members of SGI and spending time at SGI gatherings, represent a social dimension of involvement. These variables are more discriminating.

Furthermore, these two dimensions of involvement correspond to a distinction between chanting for oneself and chanting for others made by respondents during the follow-up interviews. As expressed by one member, who became active in the organization after a period of only sporadic participation in collective activities,

there's two parts to practice. You have to practice for yourself, but you have to practice for others as well. [Before] it was all practice for myself. And it got to the point where that wasn't enough. I really wanted to share these benefits with other people. I was able to bring other people to the philosophy, and that naturally led to being more involved with the organization because you need a support structure to do that.

Being involved in the organization, as opposed to chanting privately, therefore, represents not only a further degree of involvement, but also a qualitatively different way of being involved that reflects a different understanding of what the practice means. Members who were most involved in the collective life of the organization often linked their personal practice with the greater goal of world peace—a topic we will take up presently.

We now have two components representing two different ways of being involved in Soka Gakkai—the first, private involvement, being more common than the second, social involvement.[4] When the two variables in each set are combined

---

[4] To minimize the number of missing cases, cases with missing values on either of the two variables used to construct the indexes of private and social involvement were included. The value of the index (either private or social involvement) is simply the value of the one variable.

into indexes and cross-tabulated, the result resembles a Guttman scale.[5]

In a Guttman scale, the variables are related in such a way that one's location on the scale pretty much indicates how that person responded to each of the indicators making up the scale. Thus, a pole-vaulter who indicates that his best jump cleared 14 feet would have said "yes" to questions about whether he had cleared 13 feet, 12 feet, etc., but would have said "no" to having cleared 15 feet. In social survey research, the data rarely perform so neatly. It is exciting to find, therefore, that these data largely do. In this case, people who are socially involved in the organized life of the group are also privately involved. Table 13 demonstrates that out of 391 cases, only 29 (7 percent) violate the Guttman pattern—that is, are more socially involved than privately involved (the three upper right cells of Table 13). This contrasts with 188 members (48 percent) whose private involvement exceeds their social involvement.

These results thus provide a good way to classify respondents as marginal, general, or core members of SGI-USA. Those who seldom chant or study and are not involved in the social life of Soka Gakkai are called "marginal" members (the 92 persons in the three upper left cells of Table 13). At the other extreme,

Table 13. The private and social dimensions of involvement cross-tabulated (in numbers)

Private involvement	Social involvement		
	Low	Moderate	High
Low	27	13	1
Moderate	52	92	15
High	30	105	56

[5] Louis Guttman, "The Basis for Scalogram Analysis," in S. Stouffer *et al.* (eds.), *Measurement and Prediction* (Princeton: Princeton University Press, 1950).

those who score high on both dimensions of involvement are called "core" members (the 56 persons in the lower right corner of Table 13). The remainder are labeled "general" members. Table 14 describes the results of this exercise.

Table 14. Degree of involvement

Status	No.	%
Marginal	92	24
General	243	62
Core	56	14

How well does the involvement scale work? To test the validity of the involvement measure, the three categories of respondents were compared according to length of involvement, the acquisition of leadership positions, and the number of people they had introduced to Soka Gakkai. The relationships are strong and work in the expected direction. Membership status is strongly correlated with length of involvement (0.282, $p < 0.000$), the number of people the respondents had introduced to the practice (0.372, $p < 0.000$), and the amount of time spent each week speaking with non-members about SGI (0.309, $p < 0.000$).[6] Furthermore, the classification scheme predicts with notable accuracy whether respondents have held positions of leadership at various organizational levels in SGI-USA. Reading across Table 15, one will notice that the likelihood that respondents have held positions of leadership at each organizational level rises as one moves from the marginal to core members. The results are strong and significant at all levels,

---

[6] "p" represents the probability that the relationship observed in the sample is due to chance, and the correlation between the two variables in the population is zero (no relationship). Thus, a value of $p < 0.05$ means that the probability of no relationship is less than 5%. When $p < 0.000$, virtually no possibility exists that the observed relationship occurred by chance.

Table 15. Leadership positions by degree of involvement (%)

Organizational level	Marginal	General	Core	Sig.[a]
Group	45	75	89	0.000
District	26	59	84	0.000
Chapter	11	34	55	0.000
Headquarters	8	20	45	0.000
Area	3	13	27	0.002
Region	3	10	9	0.213

Note: Question 21 in the questionnaire, App. C.

[a] The uncertainty coefficient, a variation on Chi-squared, was used to evaluate significance.

except the region, in which case failure to achieve significance is probably because of the small number of respondents who have held such national offices.

A final validation of the classification scheme results from comparing the responses of core members with general and marginal members to a question pertaining to future involvement in SGI (Table 16). The survey asked respondents to indicate how likely it is that they would drop out of SGI someday. No respondents classified as core members indicated that they might drop out. Eighty percent of the core members replied that they would never stop chanting or going to group meetings. Another 16 percent indicated that this outcome was very unlikely. Comparatively, of those classified as marginal members, 7 percent indicated that they had already stopped attending meetings, though they continue to chant privately. Ten percent replied that they might drop out of Soka Gakkai someday, and 37 percent indicated that they might cut down on attendance at SGI group events, though they did not expect to stop chanting.

These data probably do not adequately capture those members of the Soka Gakkai who are currently in the process of leaving. It makes sense that people who are leaving the religion

Table 16. How likely is it that you will drop out of SGI-USA someday? (%)

Possibility of attrition	Marginal	General	Core	All
"I'll never stop chanting or going to group meetings."	29	59	80	55
"It's very unlikely that I will stop chanting or going to group meetings."	17	24	16	21
"I'll never stop chanting, though I might cut down on my attendance at meetings."	37	16	4	19
"There is a chance that I will drop out."	10	1	—	3
Has already stopped attending meetings, but still chants (volunteered).	7	—	—	2
N	89	235	56	380

Notes: Question 47 in the questionnaire, App. C.
Chi-squared = 84.806, df = 8, p <0.000

would not have taken the time to fill out a survey that took about an hour to complete. Those persons who had *already* dropped out of Soka Gakkai but whose names were included in the sample were instructed not to fill out the survey, so this group is not represented at all. Still, the data do capture a group that appears to be at risk of defection. Of the 89 marginally involved members in Table 16, 47 (12 percent of the entire sample) indicated that they might cut down on attendance or drop out of SGI someday. More will be said in Chapter 6 about why some people become very committed while others defect. For now, it is sufficient to note that the data capture currently active members at all levels of involvement, and the method used to classify members' levels of involvement appears to work very well.

What Members Chant for

Since chanting is central to Soka Gakkai religion, a closer analysis of what members chant for is in order. In Soka Gakkai, chanting for specific, conspicuous benefits is not perceived as contradictory to the ostensible goal of personal enlightenment or improving one's karma. Instead, one's external, material circumstances are viewed as an effect of one's inner, spiritual condition. It comes as no surprise, therefore, that when asked about the goals and benefits of chanting, conspicuous benefits, such as acquiring a new home, a car, success in one's career, or good health, are mentioned frequently. In fact, Soka Gakkai members are encouraged to think of such benefits as "proof" that the practice works—proof that not only serves to encourage continued practice but also to encourage others to try chanting.

But does this pattern remain constant as the Soka Gakkai members mature in their understanding of Nichiren Buddhism? Given the emphasis on the efficacy of chanting, what happens when chanting doesn't work? Is the perception of identifiable benefits critical to the maintenance of commitment over time, or do the reasons members give for their involvement in Soka Gakkai change?

Virtually all of the respondents indicated that they chanted with particular goals in mind. In an open-ended question respondents were asked to describe the goals for which they chanted. The specific goals mentioned vary from the very conspicuous to the very inconspicuous. Conspicuous goals include material rewards, such as money, new cars, homes, etc. These rewards are distinguishable from others in that the result is manifest and quantifiable. Somewhat less conspicuous benefits, but still verifiable, include psychological or physical health, and success in a career. The most inconspicuous goals include world peace, spiritual enlightenment and faith, and better karma. Table 17 describes the frequency with which respondents reported chanting for each of these kinds of goal. Up to three

Table 17. Goals of chanting (%)

Goals mentioned	Marginal	General	Core	All
Conspicuous, material goals:				
Financial rewards	27	18	14	19
Material rewards (new house, car, etc.)	14	23	22	21
Conspicuous, non-material goals:				
Psychological well-being, confidence	18	11	14	13
Physical health	26	26	35	27
Career success	39	53	41	48
Better relationships	47	39	37	40
Inconspicuous goals:				
Spiritual enlightenment, faith	1	2	4	2
Human revolution, karma	4	6	8	6
World peace	1	2	2	2
N	74	208	49	336

Notes. Question 26 in the questionnaire, App. C. Columns add up to more than 100% because up to three different goals for each respondent are included in the table.

different goals were coded and included in this table, so the numbers add to more than 100 percent.

Most often, the goals mentioned were articulated as conspicuous but non-material goals. The goal most frequently mentioned reflects the concern that we would expect to dominate the minds of upwardly mobile young Americans—success in a career. Forty-eight percent of the respondents said that they had chanted for success in their career. Career success is followed by concerns about personal relationships, mentioned by 40 percent, and physical health, 27 percent. These concerns are no doubt typical of Americans in the prime of their lives. Although career success is clearly related to a desire for material rewards—having money and being able to purchase things such as houses or cars—it is telling that these rewards are secondary to careers in the minds of SGI-USA members. To these Soka Gakkai members, chanting is not perceived as a magical ritual used to make the external world conform to one's desires. Instead, it appears to be perceived as a means of empowering the self—a way to be successful, healthy, and happy in relationships—from which other kinds of rewards follow. As mentioned in Chapter 1, members may joke about chanting to win the lottery, but the understanding of how chanting works is much more complex. Chanting is understood by most members as a means of self-improvement, rather than as magic, an understanding largely consistent with the official belief.

Note that such inconspicuous goals as spiritual enlightenment, better karma, and world peace make only a minor appearance as goals for which members chant. When asked what benefits SGI members have *actually experienced*, however, these inconspicuous goals are mentioned more frequently (Table 18). In a question similar to the one about the *goals* of chanting,

Table 18. Benefits of chanting (%)

Benefits mentioned	Marginal	General	Core	All
Conspicuous material goals:				
Financial rewards	7	4	4	5
Material rewards (new house, car, etc.)	1	1	2	1
Conspicuous non-material goals:				
Psychological well-being, confidence	53	50	50	50
Physical health	13	12	15	12
Career success	3	6	9	6
Better relationships	9	17	17	16
Inconspicuous goals:				
Spiritual enlightenment, faith	16	11	11	12
Human revolution, karma	20	26	30	25
N	76	218	54	353

Notes: Question 25 in the questionnaire, App. C.

respondents were asked to describe *benefits they had actually experienced* as a result of chanting. Twenty-five percent mentioned "human revolution," an improvement in their character or "life condition." Only 6 percent, however, reported having chanted with this goal in mind. Respondents were nearly five times more likely to mention spiritual enlightenment and faith as results they had experienced than they were to say that they had chanted for these goals. Mentioned much less frequently as benefits experienced as a result of chanting are career success, better relationships, and physical health. The most frequently mentioned benefits are confidence and other aspects of psychological well-being. Most dramatic in the shift from goals *desired* to goals *achieved* is in the category of conspicuous material goals; 40 percent chanted for such goals, but only 6 percent reported success.

The theory of religion developed by Rodney Stark and William S. Bainbridge provides a helpful way to understand why the benefits identified by members differ so dramatically from the goals for which they report chanting.[7] These sociologists argue that it is in human nature to seek rewards and avoid costs. However, some rewards are quite scarce and not available to everyone in a society. Because of this fact of life, people create compensators, defined as "the belief that a reward will be obtained in the distant future or in some other context which cannot be immediately verified."[8] While rewards can be experienced and verified, compensators require faith. Religions, by the Stark and Bainbridge definition, are organizations that specialize in the production of compensators. In the case of Soka Gakkai, despite the emphasis on proof that the practice works, such compensators as better karma, confidence, peace of mind, and a sense of spiritual awareness (inconspicuous goals) are sufficient to sustain commitment when chanting does not have the results

---

[7] Rodney Stark and William Sims Bainbridge, *The Future of Religion: Secularization, Revival, and Cult Formation* (Berkeley: University of California Press, 1985).

[8] Ibid. 6.

for which members had hoped (conspicuous goals). In a sense, these compensators give Soka Gakkai members reason to believe that chanting is helpful, even when the results initially desired are not always forthcoming. Confidence that a continued improvement in one's "life condition" will make it possible to buy a new car in the future is sufficient compensation for the fact that, in the meantime, one must continue driving the old one.

It is notable that only minor (and statistically insignificant) differences emerge in the goals and benefits mentioned by people who differ in degree of involvement. This finding does not mean, however, that the experience of benefits has no relationship to involvement. Differences do show up: (1) in the way members describe what the practice means in their personal lives, and (2) in the ways that members interpret the apparent disparity between the goals for which they chant and the actual results.

The Meaning of Chanting

The most dramatic difference in the way respondents described what the practice of Soka Gakkai Buddhism means in their personal lives appears when the responses of active members are compared with those who have dropped out. Compare the following comments:

Active Members

I've learned to . . . take the most positive action through chanting. . . My father [who also chants] used to be, in his younger years, not really abusive, not physically abusive, but more emotionally abusive and just a really insecure person. [He] is now compassionate. He's much more aware of his actions.

The practice is very much about how we live our lives, and we chant to polish our character and to challenge our lives and to grow. . . . We try not to be effect-oriented. We try to be cause-oriented. We try to think about, "What am I putting out? What am I doing?"

One thing to understand about chanting is that it's not really magic. It's really a means to unlock subjective wisdom in your own life that you can use . . . your talents, your ability, your wisdom to solve a problem.

Whatever your goal is, that's fine. You chant about those things. And through that process, you elevate your life state at its core, so you can purify your life and say, "OK, I want this car," but the car is really not the goal. Enlightenment or happiness is the goal. Then you find out . . . maybe I need to get a job. Maybe I need to be more responsible with my money. Maybe I need to save some money. Maybe I need to learn how to buy a car. . . . It all starts with our own determination that, "I'm going to make something happen."

The big obstacle for everybody is to get over the idea that when I chant, some agency outside myself is going to present me with what I'm chanting for. When in fact, the actual practice is quite the opposite. One chants and then one acts.

You may be confused about where to go in your life. It's like driving along in the fog, and you don't know where you are. But when the fog lifts, you can see perfectly well, and then it's clear. You know where to go and what to do. And that's the effect you get from chanting.

Drop-outs

I would chant in a situation of uncertainty or tension, and it seemed to have a calming effect. I suffered from a bipolar disorder—I was manic-depressive. And chanting had the effect of helping me find balance, harmony, where my ups weren't so up and my downs weren't quite as bad as they had been.

My life was pretty tumultuous at the time. Things have worked themselves out since then, so I don't know whether you could say that was a benefit of the chanting or that was just a cyclic progression of life.

It doesn't seem to matter whether you're chanting or not. Nothing makes a difference. Things go the way they go. . . . I do have a connection with [chanting], and I always come back. And I always enjoy it when I do it. But then, I guess I start questioning its worth.

Not only were the active members of Soka Gakkai more willing than the drop-outs to attribute positive experiences to the effect of chanting; their responses demonstrate a qualitatively different understanding of how chanting works. The active members found that chanting helped them to take responsibility for the circumstances in their lives. Chanting, for these members, helped them to gain clarity about what actions they could take to make changes in their lives. The drop-outs, conversely, spoke of chanting as if it were supposed to work independently of their own efforts. When the desired changes did not occur, therefore, they simply assumed that chanting doesn't work. When they did experience improvements in their lives, they interpreted these as things just working themselves out.

In contrast to the descriptions of chanting by drop-outs, those offered by current members who appear to be wavering in their commitment to SGI-USA resembled very closely those of the most involved members. Both core and marginal members emphasized changes in their outlook on life and their ability to take responsibility for their own happiness. In fact, most of the wavering members were sufficiently convinced of the benefits of chanting that they did not expect ever to stop chanting, although they questioned their commitment to participating in the organization. This suggests that, while the perception of benefits is a necessary precondition to involvement, other kinds of experience determine how involved in the organization people will become.

How Members Interpreted Failed Results

Seventy-one percent of the survey respondents indicated that they had chanted for a goal not realized. As we would expect from the above results, the goals most frequently mentioned as unrealized were conspicuous: better relationships (35 percent), career success (21 percent), and financial rewards (12 percent). Respondents were then asked to describe *why* the goal was not realized. Four possible responses were given from which respondents could choose: (1) The goal was incompatible with my lifelong happiness/Buddhahood; (2) Chanting doesn't work for some goals; (3) I probably need to go through my human revolution before I'll achieve that goal; or (4) I wasn't practicing correctly (Table 19).

Table 19. Why chanting does not always work (%)

Reason	Marginal	General	Core	All
The goal was incompatible with my lifelong happiness/ Buddhahood	22	25	19	23
Chanting doesn't work for some goals	12	1	—	4
I probably need to go through my human revolution before I'll achieve that goal	24	37	59	36
I wasn't practicing correctly	10	7	9	8
Other reasons	31	31	13	29
N	67	154	32	253

Notes: Question 28 in the questionnaire, App. C.
Chi-squared = 27.110, df = 8, p < 0.01

The first explanation suggests that the goal would not have been beneficial and therefore it was unrealized. For instance, one respondent explained that he had chanted for money to buy drugs, a goal incompatible with his long-term well-being. In fact, in a follow-up interview, this respondent indicated that not achieving the goal of having money to buy drugs turned out to be an unexpected benefit: "By the time I got to the point where I was able to get drugs, I didn't want them anymore." The second response raises the possibility that chanting does not always work. The third explanation locates the reason in the individual's karma, suggesting that a certain amount of personal growth is required before the goal will be realized. This explanation is the most consistent with Soka Gakkai doctrine. The final answer asserts that chanting works, but only if practiced consistently and correctly; when chanting does not result in the benefits expected, therefore, it is probably because members were not chanting enough, or without the required concentration.

The doctrinal (third) response is the one most frequently chosen to explain failed results (36 percent; Table 19). The first option was the next most common: the goal was incompatible with the individual's long-term happiness and development (23 percent). This response also reflects Soka Gakkai doctrine. In other words, most of the respondents interpreted failed results in terms of their individual karma, or life-condition, which is still in the process of development. Only a few respondents entertained the possibility that chanting sometimes doesn't work, or that it works only when practiced correctly. Notably, the majority of respondents who reported unrealized goals said they would continue chanting for these goals. The only exceptions were those who said they thought that the goal was probably incompatible with their long-term happiness.

Note, however, that degree of involvement is related to differences in the way members interpret failed results. Those members who are most involved in SGI are more likely to give the response that conforms to Soka Gakkai doctrine. Seventy-eight percent of core members and 62 percent of general members, but only 46 percent of marginal members, select the first or third answer. None of the respondents classified as core members said that chanting sometimes does not work. Marginal members were the most likely to entertain this possibility.

These results suggest that, despite what might be described as a materialistic orientation of Soka Gakkai Buddhism, what the religion chiefly offers is not specific, conspicuous rewards, but compensators such as faith, a sense of personal happiness, and confidence. These results are constant at all levels of involvement, suggesting that the experience of demonstrable rewards is not necessary for the development and sustenance of commitment, SGI rhetoric notwithstanding. As members become more involved in the religion, however, their understanding of how chanting works, and why it sometimes does not work, reflects a more orthodox understanding of Soka Gakkai beliefs.

The Goal of World Peace

If it is not the experience of verifiable benefits that serves to sustain involvement, what does? Even if the respondents to the survey could identify specific verifiable results from chanting, there remains no necessary reason for participation in the collective life of the organization. Chanting is understood as a means of unlocking the individual's inner Buddha wisdom for application in their daily lives, and the practice is believed to work even when chanting and study are done privately. However, SGI promotes another goal that serves to refocus attention away from the self and may work to stimulate a sense of collective identity—the goal of world peace.

In Soka Gakkai Buddhism, world peace is promoted at three levels. First, individual enlightenment is believed to promote inner peace and self-confidence. Second, these individuals in their daily lives make positive "causes" in their families and communities for harmonious social relations. Third, the organization and its leaders engage in efforts to promote peace at the national and international levels. Every year, for instance, Soka Gakkai delegates present a peace proposal to the United Nations on behalf of President Ikeda, and meet regularly with national leaders to promote dialogue and cross-cultural understanding. Wilson and Dobbelaere suggest that the goal of world peace, together with the promotion of art and culture, and ecological conservation, provide "corporate ends which bind members in commitment to higher purposes" beyond self-satisfaction, adding a social dimension to the practice.[9] The 1997 SGI-USA Membership Survey supports this hypothesis.

Core members are twice as likely as marginal members to say that the goal of world peace is very realistic (Table 20). No core members said that they thought this goal was unrealistic. By comparison, 17 percent of the respondents classified as marginal said that they thought the goal of world peace was not very realistic or not at all realistic.

[9] Wilson and Dobbelaere, *Time to Chant*, 229.

Table 20. How realistic is the goal of world peace? (%)

Reply	Marginal	General	Core	All
Very realistic	39	61	79	59
Pretty realistic	43	30	20	32
Not very realistic	14	6	2	7
Not realistic	3	2	—	2
Don't know (volunteered)	1	—	—	1
N	89	237	56	382

Notes: Question 41 in the questionnaire, App. C.
Chi-squared = 26.477, df = 8, p <0.01

Hardly any respondents indicated that they thought chanting alone was sufficient to bring about this goal. In their minds, other actions are necessary, though members at all levels of involvement said they thought Soka Gakkai's efforts were essential. Most of the respondents were able to mention something they were doing themselves to promote this goal, the most common being working to improve their own lives (33 percent), setting a good example for their children or other people (19 percent), and introducing others to SGI (18 percent). More telling with regard to involvement were the respondents' answers to a question about what SGI was doing as an organization to promote this goal (Table 21). Core members were more likely to celebrate the international efforts of SGI and efforts to promote cross-cultural awareness and dialogue. The marginal members more often gave generic responses, such as "education," without specifying any further. Marginal members were more likely than general or core members to say they simply didn't know.

It was noted earlier that in personal interviews with SGI-USA members, the most active members commonly linked the experience of personal growth with the collective goal of world peace. Compare the responses of these active members (both core and general members) with some who appear to be waver-

Table 21. Besides chanting, what is SGI doing as an organization to promote world peace? (%)

Activities mentioned	Marginal	General	Core	All
International leadership, involvement in the UN	13	23	27	21
Promoting cross-cultural dialogue	17	15	33	18
Spreading Nichiren Buddhism	18	12	—	12
Education and cultural efforts	21	20	17	20
Nothing	—	1	—	1
Don't know	6	3	—	3
Other	26	26	23	25
N	78	214	52	344

Notes: Question 44 in the questionnaire, App. C.
Chi-squared = 25.811, df = 12, $p < 0.05$.

ing in their dedication to SGI-USA (mostly marginal members):

Active members

We chant that all those other aspects of being a human being are in rhythm with "Nam-myoho-renge-kyo," and they can be used for our greatest actions, for what we call our mission—our mission to do good, to help bring about world peace, and to touch people's lives one by one. So somebody might use anger to stand up for justice.

If we have enough people in the world chanting, we can create a society where things can be resolved in a peaceful way. I've been a member for over twenty years, and I've read a lot of material, and I really believe that the chanting and the philosophy are beneficial and they're having a positive impact on the world as a whole.

That is the whole idea of *kosen-rufu*—basically, the world as I know it is generated by my action and my beliefs and my willingness to take responsibility for that. . . . There is no retreating from the reality that you live in a social world. . . . Because we do live in a world, we have a commitment to that world and a commitment to improving that world.

It's a very lotus-like fact that we do exhibit beauty in such a muddy, funky swamp as this world.

Our potential for positive things—for growth and for development and for constructive capability—is largely dependent on the condition of our lives; the life-condition that we're in. To the extent that we can nourish and develop the Buddha condition that exists within our life, then we're expanding our capability. Practicing for other people enables us to do that—to overcome our lesser self and open up our broader self. By overcoming the self-centeredness, the egotism, by caring and practicing for others, we're expanding our lives beyond our own self-centered, egotistical aspect of our lives. We're able to grow. Our Buddha nature—our Buddha condition, our life, you could say— expands.

Wavering members

When I sense that something is not the way I want it in my life, I chant for people who I think may be affecting what's happening to me, but not for any particular change with what's happening in my life. It's just for the people who are involved—either causing difficulty or discomfort at the time.

I see a real change in myself, and an opportunity to change. And then, to work for *kosen-rufu*—I like the idea very much.

I think any type of organization that is promoting world peace and culture, if you can get involved, it really does expand your life and your mindset into being less selfish and to helping other people.

The most involved members quite clearly think of improving their own lives—notably, their personal character and sense of responsibility for others—as a means of promoting world peace. In the minds of members who are wavering in their commitment, the link between personal happiness and world peace is more tenuous.

The goal of world peace and SGI's promotion of ecological awareness evidently do serve an integrative function, as Wilson and Dobbelaere suggest. Of course the causal direction is questionable. That is, it makes sense to think that the more involved members would be more likely to think of their practice in terms of collective goals. It is also reasonable to think that those members who are most concerned about world peace would be drawn to greater levels of involvement in an organization involved in world peace efforts. At this point, it is sufficient to note that the two variables are related, suggesting that learning to think about one's own practice in terms of world peace is one factor related to involvement. It makes further sense, therefore, to expect that core members would be more engaged in efforts to recruit others to join Soka Gakkai. This is, in fact, the case.

The survey included a question asking whether respondents had been active in introducing others to Soka Gakkai. While close to 90 percent of all the respondents indicated that they had been at least somewhat active in this regard, core members were more than three times as likely to say they had been "very active" recruiting others to the practice, 66 percent choosing that response, compared to 19 percent of the marginal members. The number of people respondents had introduced to Soka Gakkai also reflects this pattern (Table 22). Core members reported introducing more people to Soka Gakkai than did marginal members. All core members said they had introduced at least one person to the practice, while 28 percent of the marginal members said they had introduced no one. At the other extreme, about 8 in 10 core members had introduced 5 or more others to SGI (most claiming to have introduced 16 or more), whereas only 4 in 10 marginal members had introduced that many (most fewer than 16). Furthermore, core members may be more effective in recruitment efforts than others. When asked whether the people they had introduced to SGI-USA are still active, the modal response for all members was "less than half remain active." However, 35 percent of marginal members replied "all have dropped out," while only 5 percent of core members gave this response.

This commitment to Soka Gakkai and its efforts to achieve world peace does not, however, translate into religious

Table 22. Number of people respondent has introduced to Soka Gakkai (%)

No. of people	Marginal	General	Core	All
None	28	8	0	11
1	2	4	2	3
2–4	32	25	20	26
5–15	24	37	35	33
16 or more	15	27	44	26
N	89	237	55	381

Notes: Question 32 in the questionnaire, App. C.
Chi-squared = 48.762, df = 8, p <0.000.

exclusivism or intolerance of other religions. This finding is surprising, since the religion's founder, Nichiren, showed little tolerance for religious diversity. He described other religions as spiritual "poison" and the teaching of false doctrines as one of the main causes of social problems. Nor was Soka Gakkai, in its early, post-World War II years all that committed to full religious liberty. Such exclusiveness is not evident, however, among SGI-USA members. When asked whether cooperating with other religions, such as Christianity, Judaism, or Islam, in promoting world peace would compromise Soka Gakkai's commitment to the teachings of Nichiren, the vast majority of respondents (82 percent) said, "no." When the question is focused specifically on other forms of Buddhism, the results are the same. Seventy-three percent of the respondents said that cooperation with other forms of Buddhism would not compromise Soka Gakkai's commitment to the truths espoused by Nichiren. These responses are constant across the several levels of involvement.

This tolerance issue may explain why several of the members are wavering in their commitment to Soka Gakkai's organized activities; they cited other member's *intolerance* of other religions as one of the primary reasons they were thinking of dropping out. One such person, for instance, was offended when his

Catholic girlfriend was exposed to anti-Catholic sentiments at a Soka Gakkai meeting. Another dropped out after he was discouraged from seeking inspiration by studying other religious traditions. While most members of SGI-USA express tolerance of other religions, then, those few who do not can cause disaffection among others.

Feelings about the Schism

The different understandings of how chanting works and SGI's role in the promotion of peace are related to members' attitudes about the split with the Nichiren Shoshu priests. Core members were nearly three times more likely to say that SGI is better off since the split (70 percent) than marginal members (28 percent). Marginal members were more likely to say that the split harmed SGI (29 percent), or that the schism made no difference whatsoever (39 percent). Members who are the most sold on SGI's organized efforts for reform are probably more likely to see the split as relieving SGI of an undue burden on resources that could be focused on efforts other than supporting the priesthood. The priesthood, after all, has had little to do with SGI's efforts to promote art, education, and political reform. To SGI members, world peace will be achieved by spiritually enlightened individuals working in the world rather than through sacraments performed by priests removed from the world. Core members, who understand this position best, are more likely, therefore, to perceive the split with the priesthood as liberating Soka Gakkai to pursue its progressive program of reform without the restraints imposed by a conservative priesthood.

Still, the schism did have an impact, and often in very personal ways. One woman, for instance, related that animosity between the two groups cost her a very close friendship with a woman who followed her husband to the temple:

At the time when she went to the temple, I became pregnant with my son . . . and I needed her friendship. And at the time that [her friendship] would have meant most to me, she withdrew. . . .Whenever I tried to reach out to her and be a friend to her—despite the fact that I obviously didn't agree with her choice—her husband was just very abrasive and said, "don't call my wife anymore" And as a result of that, I think I really lost a dear friend. . . . I really knew that sticking with the Gakkai was right, but it was a difficult choice for me to make because I felt that it came at a price.

Several of the marginally involved members expressed dissatisfaction with the way Soka Gakkai leaders handled the priesthood issue:

I think that instead of looking and saying, "How can we grow" because of this, we're just constantly hearing about [Nikken]. I know he's not a good man, but it seems like a rivalry between Nikken and President Ikeda.

Since that happened, we seem to be devoting a lot of time and energy to fighting between the two groups—priesthood and the lay organization. It's discouraging.

[I decided to cut back on participation] because of the way the leaders in my city were responding to the priesthood issue. . . . And it was in a slanderous way—that the high priest is an evil person. It was all negative, and according to the *Gosho*, we're not supposed to do that. . . . I stopped subscribing in 1993 because the *World Tribune* was too negative toward the priesthood. . . . I wish this issue could be resolved. I wish the two men would get together and talk this thing over, because it's divided our members throughout the world and that's bad.

Right now, they—maybe I should say, "we," since I still practice—are very condemning of the priests. Not the priests, but the head priest. They've even said that he's evil and all. I really don't believe in good and evil. I think it's just different. Nothing is black and white. . . . So I don't like that much—having big campaigns to get somebody.

In brief, while the schism itself did not cause a great number of members to question their commitment to Soka Gakkai, the way Soka Gakkai leaders handled the controversy bothered some. To these members, antagonistic statements made by SGI leaders about Nikken and the priesthood generally were inconsistent with SGI's stated values of promoting peace.

In Conclusion

Although these data suggest some possible reasons for variation in degrees of involvement, our primary concern in this chapter has been to *describe* involvement and how core members differ from the general and marginal members. The measure of involvement has a strong association with: (1) the number of people introduced to Soka Gakkai Buddhism, (2) whether these members have held leadership positions, and (3) how members understand chanting. In regard to the latter, the explanation members give for failed results is most revealing. Although there is very little variation in the goals for which members chant and the way members describe the benefits of chanting, core members are less likely to entertain the possibility that chanting doesn't work. They are more likely to perceive conspicuous benefits as a consequence of the individual's changing life-condition, and, therefore, to accept the perception of internal changes as compensation for more immediate rewards.

Perhaps the most notable finding is the variation in attitudes about the collective goal of world peace. Core SGI-USA members are more likely to believe that world peace is possible. They appear, as well, to be better informed about SGI's organized efforts in pursuit of that goal.

Furthermore, these different understandings of how chanting works, and the role of SGI in the development of world peace, are linked with members' feelings about the schism with the priesthood. Those members who perceive the necessity of collective reform efforts are more likely to have felt the tension of affiliation with an established priesthood. To them, the schism did not harm the situation of Soka Gakkai, but may have improved it. Indeed, the perceived inconsistency between SGI's stated goals of promoting peace and the way Soka Gakkai leaders handled the priesthood issue may have caused more members to question their commitment to SGI-USA than did the schism itself.

II

SGI-USA
Its Converts

4

Supply-Side Influences on the Development of SGI-USA

URRENT sociological wisdom suggests that three factors influence the destiny of a religion entering a new social environment: (1) the degree to which that environment is religiously unregulated and thus open to religious competition, (2) decisions made and actions taken by a religious organization itself regarding how it will deliver its message, and (3) the degree to which that message is an appealing alternative to the religions already available to the society's members.

The first and second factors combined form what is called the "supply-side" theory of the organizational growth and decline of religions. What flexibility is a religious organization allowed, and what does it do with that flexibility? The impact of these factors on the development of SGI-USA is discussed here in Chapter 4. The third factor could be called the "demand-side" theory; it is discussed in Chapter 5. Chapter 6 then combines these perspectives into an overall portrait of religious accommodation and conversion.

Supply-side thinking about religious change represents a relatively new development in the study of religion. Drawing on the metaphor of the religious market, supply-side theorists assert that religion is "an object of choice and production."[1] And religious organizations and religious leaders are portrayed as "producers who choose the characteristics of their product

---

[1] Finke and Iannaccone, "Supply-Side Explanations for Religious Change," 28.

and the means of marketing it."[2] The impact of supply-side factors is clearly illustrated in the case of Soka Gakkai. Although Soka Gakkai was present in the United States from as early as the 1940s, it was not until two decades later that conditions were suited to the development of an organization there. A number of social changes beginning in the 1960s allowed the spread of Buddhism generally in the United States. SGI-USA played the newly opened market wisely, adopting a low-tension position close enough to the American mainstream religious culture to be a realistic alternative for those who encountered the religion, but unique enough to maintain its distinctive appeal. As a result, SGI-USA and those who decided to join it have experienced minimal conflict in the United States.

Social and Religious Change in the United States

Perhaps the most significant event leading to the development of Soka Gakkai in America was the election of Daisaku Ikeda as president of the organization in Japan. Following the example of his predecessor, Toda, who had successfully fulfilled his goal of bringing 750,000 new members to the faith, Ikeda made a commitment to the continuing growth of the Soka Gakkai. However, Ikeda's vision for the organization was less parochial than that of President Toda. While Toda focused his efforts on organizational growth in Japan, Ikeda envisioned the planting of Soka Gakkai chapters worldwide. In 1960, shortly after his election, Ikeda made a visit to the United States to found the first overseas chapter of the Nichiren Shoshu Soka Gakkai. He spoke words of encouragement to those Japanese members living in the United States, telling them that the spread of Soka Gakkai in America would be the next chapter in the story of *kosen-rufu*, the enlightenment of the world through Nichiren Buddhism.

[2] Finke and Iannaccone, "Supply-Side Explanations for Religious Change," 28.

Mostly the Japanese wives of American military men, many of these early members had maintained their practice in isolation from other Soka Gakkai members and without the benefit of priestly services and guidance. Now, in preparation for President Ikeda's visit, they were encouraged to begin meeting together in small groups. From its origin in the United States, therefore, Soka Gakkai was composed primarily of female laity. Although in Japan these women would be excluded from positions of leadership, necessity demanded that they play key roles in the development of the organization in the United States. Rarely in the spotlight, these quiet leaders were the driving forces behind the initial efforts to recruit new members in the United States.

Despite the dedication of these early members, growth was slow for most of the first decade. Barriers of language and culture inhibited growth. Recent immigrants from Japan themselves, many of these women had difficulty with the English language. This meant that recruitment efforts were targeted largely toward other Japanese immigrants, most of whom were also women. The over-representation of women in Soka Gakkai in the early years was problematic for an organization that, modeled on the organization in Japan, limited roles of leadership to men. In the USA, the men needed to develop the organization were lacking.

The absence of men during the early years of SGI in the United States reflects US immigration policies at that time. Immigration restrictions passed earlier in the century—during a period of Anglo-Protestant nativism in America—prevented the immigration of Japanese men to the United States. Japanese were admitted to the United States only as the spouses or children of American citizens. This policy had the effect of limiting immigration from Japan, and other Asian countries, to women married to American military men.

It is no accident, then, that real growth of the Soka Gakkai in the United States did not begin until five years after the founding of an American branch of the organization. In 1965,

US President Johnson rescinded the Exclusion Act, making it easier for people from Japan to immigrate to the United States. In raw numbers, the new immigration policy had only modest effect. Immigration from Japan rose from 3,180 in 1965 to 4,457 in 1970, and leveled off at 4,000 to 4,500 per year through the 1980s.[3] The rate of immigration from Japan, therefore, reveals no huge rush. The demographic character-istics of these immigrants, however, changed dramatically after 1965, and this change had a profound impact on the develop-ment of SGI-USA.

The United States Department of Justice, Immigration and Naturalization Service reports annually the number and characteristics of new immigrants to the United States. Table 23

Table 23. Demographics of Japanese immigrants to the United States (%)

Year	Women	Professionals	Housewives/ dependents
1965	86	4	90
1970	73	15	74
1975	66	15	68
1979	64	18	63
1985	62	16	64
1990	(59)	18	60
1994	69	20	66

Note: Data on the gender and occupational characteristics of immigrants by coun-try of origin were missing for 1980. The 1979 data were used instead. In 1990, data on the gender of immigrants by country of origin were missing. These data were not available again until 1992, so the 1992 data are reported in the first column. Immigration data for 1995 were not yet available (US Department of Justice, Immigration and Naturalization Service, *Annual Reports* for 1965, 1970, 1975 (1966, 1971, 1976); *Statistical Yearbooks* for 1979, 1985, 1990, 1993 (n.d., 1986, 1991, 1994)).

[3] US Department of Justice, Immigration and Naturalization Service, *Annual Report of the Immigration and Naturalization Service* (Washington: Government Printing Office, 1965, 1970).

shows the demographic characteristics of Japanese immigrants from 1965 to 1994. Though women still outnumber men two to one, the proportion of female immigrants from Japan dropped from 86 percent in 1965 to around two-thirds a decade later. More important, from 1965 to 1970, the number of professionals (managers, executives, entrepreneurs, doctors, etc.) among the Japanese immigrants grew fivefold and has continued to grow since that time. Meanwhile, the percentage of Japanese immigrants classified as dependents (housewives, children, and parents who are unemployed) has declined.

Those Soka Gakkai members among the Japanese immigrants who arrived in the United States after 1965, therefore, were more likely to have attributes needed for leadership in the developing organization. So, too, would those immigrants who, after arriving in the United States, joined SGI-USA as a means of maintaining ethnic contacts. Beyond resolving the obvious problem of a gendered organizational hierarchy, the better-educated recent immigrants were more likely to speak English and to be in occupations that would bring them into daily contact with non-Japanese Americans. The presence of such persons in Soka Gakkai has no doubt contributed to a positive public image and has given Soka Gakkai access to a very different pool of potential recruits than was the case in the 1960s.

The impact of these changing demographics can be observed in the rapid transformation of the characteristics of converts to SGI. The earlier immigrant members were practically limited in their recruitment efforts to other Japanese-Americans and people in their immediate families. This situation accounts for the concentration of people associated with the military as of 1968. As noted in Chapter 2, from 1968 to the early 1970s, when David Snow conducted his research, the proportion of converts associated with the military dropped from 41 percent to 9 percent.[4] As Japanese immigrants to the USA came

---

[4] Snow, *Shakubuku*.

increasingly from the professional class of workers, so too did American converts to SGI. Thus, the new "supply" of Japanese immigrants employed in professional and technical occupations may partially explain the concentration of SGI-USA members in the "new class" occupations. Not only did the post-1965 immigrants bring skills that were needed for the internal development of the organization, but they also gave Soka Gakkai access to a different pool of potential recruits.

The typical pattern of SGI growth in America, as described by Jane Hurst, demonstrates still further the impact of immigration.[5] The pattern begins when a core group of Japanese immigrants organize discussion meetings for themselves, and then begin to invite family members, friends, coworkers, and, in the early days, strangers recruited through *shakubuku* campaigns. Even today, Soka Gakkai Buddhism is found primarily in metropolitan areas where there are large numbers of Japanese immigrants, notably Los Angeles, San Francisco, and New York. While it is difficult to estimate what the actual numbers might be, it seems reasonable to think that a certain critical mass of Japanese immigrants in an area is a necessary precondition for the development of a new Soka Gakkai chapter.

The new immigration policies clearly, therefore, had an impact on the spread of Soka Gakkai in America. However, the religious "market" was opening in other ways, as well. Americans had been awakening, in the decades leading up to the 1960s, to the reality of religious pluralism. Unlike the earlier periods of religious ferment, no new consensus emerged from the crisis of meaning that attended social change in the twentieth century. Instead, the awakening of the twentieth century was an awakening to pluralism that resulted in a further "disestablishment" of Protestantism.

Historian Martin Marty chronicles the Protestant struggle in the early decades of the twentieth century to maintain unity in the face of religious pluralism, modern nationalism, and the

---

[5] Hurst, "Nichiren Shoshu Soka Gakkai".

realities of life in industrial society.[6] However, attempts to unify seemed only to promote further fragmentation. By the 1930s it was becoming clear that conflict over the proper interpretation of the Bible had led to a permanent rift in the Protestant churches. Meanwhile, new lines of conflict emerged over issues of public morality, such as the sale and use of alcohol, relations between labor and business, as well as race relations. These conflicts added complexity to the existing lines of religious division. Hopes for a new Protestant consensus were dashed.

By the 1960s, the implications of pluralism were seen in several ways. Robert Bellah noted a change in civil religious discourse.[7] American ingenuity, hard work, and dedication to the enlightenment principles of liberty gradually took the place of Providence as the source of national identity and hope for America's future. At the same time, new patterns of religious mobility signaled the development of a more radical level of religious individualism and autonomy.[8] While collectively the nation moved to explore new frontiers internationally, and even in outer space, many religious individuals were turning inward, seeking a new spiritual center in the empowered, enlightened, and realized self. This "third disestablishment" clearly did much to open the religious market to new competitors.

Indeed, this awakening to pluralism may underlie the further deregulation of religion by the state. Hammond argues that increased religious pluralism forced the Supreme Court to clarify the meaning of the free exercise and establishment clauses of the Constitution.[9] In a pattern consistent with the

---

[6] Martin Marty, *Modern American Religion*, i: *The Irony of it All, 1893–1919*; ii: *The Noise of Conflict* (Chicago: University of Chicago Press, 1986, 1991). See also, Robert Handy, *A Christian America*, 2nd edn. (New York: Oxford University Press, 1984).

[7] Robert Bellah, "Civil Religion in America," *Daedalus*, 96/1 (1967), 1–20.

[8] Phillip E. Hammond, *Religion and Personal Autonomy: The Third Disestablishment in America* (Columbia, SC: University of South Carolina Press, 1992); Roof, *Generation of Seekers*.

[9] Phillip E. Hammond, *With Liberty for All* (Louisville, Ky.: Westminster John Knox Press, 1998).

new religious individualism, the Supreme Court has increasingly stretched its definition of religion to include individual conscience. This broader definition of religion, and what qualifies therefore for Constitutional protection from intervention by the government, amounts to a further deregulation of the religious market.

These changes—the further disestablishment of Protestant religion and the associated deregulation of the religious market—made the United States a more hospitable environment for new religious alternatives to emerge and prosper. However, they did not favor Soka Gakkai uniquely. Other new religions in the United States at the same time did less well than Soka Gakkai, often experiencing spurts of growth and then sudden decline, but rarely achieving organizational stability. For an explanation of the performance of the Soka Gakkai relative to these other new religions, therefore, we must explore other possibilities.

Organizational Tactics and Positioning

Much sociological research on religion has focused on the ways that organizational practices express creeds and codes, the preservation and promotion of which are the organization's reasons for existing. Only rarely, however, as in the case of religious ritual, is the expression of creeds and codes the sole purpose of such practices. More often, practices are aimed at achieving particular ends—such as gaining members, feeding the hungry, maintaining a budget, or consoling the afflicted—and will be maintained to the degree the practices are perceived as successful. Furthermore, religious organizations do not exist in isolation. They exist within societal fields where certain rules and expectations, institutionalized to greater or lesser degrees, apply. The success of organizational practices, therefore, will depend not only on rational considerations of utility, but also on conformity with norms and expectations.

Organizations that violate what are perceived to be the rules of fair play are likely to be perceived as illegitimate and are less likely, therefore, to attract new members or sustain the commitment of new recruits. Considerations of legitimacy are more important to *religious* organizations, which supply a product the quality of which is not immediately evident.[10] The success of an automobile manufacturer, for instance, depends largely on the quality of its automobiles relative to their price. A manufacturer who produces poor-quality automobiles is not likely to succeed. When the thing being produced is largely inconspicuous, however, such as education or religion, organizational success depends more heavily on the organization's reputation as a legitimate supplier.

The perception of legitimacy presents an even greater challenge to *new* suppliers of religion. Few would bother to question the legitimacy of the Presbyterian or Catholic Church, for example. However, suspicions abound over the legitimacy of new religions such as the Unification Church (Moonies), Scientology, or the Divine Light Mission. Much of the reason for SGI-USA's success stems from the way it negotiated this challenge of legitimacy.

By the time Soka Gakkai began seriously to organize for growth in the United States, it had already achieved, in Japan, a working organizational form. By utilitarian criteria, such as membership growth and mobilization of economic and social resources, the organizational model of the Soka Gakkai in Japan was working very well. There, the organization was growing rapidly in new members and capital resources. Therefore, in the United States, the Soka Gakkai would have been tempted to replicate the Japanese model, which, in a sense, was the case during the early years of SGI-USA's existence.

The problems to be experienced by Soka Gakkai in America, however, were not problems of utility but problems of legitimacy. Even in Japan, where association with an established

[10] John Meyer and Brian Rowan, "Institutionalized Organizations: Formal Structure as Myth and Ceremony," in Walter Powell and Paul DiMaggio (eds.), *The New Institutionalism in Organizational Analysis* (Chicago: University of Chicago Press, 1991), 41–62.

Nichiren sect enhanced Soka Gakkai's credibility, problems of legitimacy had hindered the organization's performance. Aggressive proselytizing, massive public demonstrations, and Soka Gakkai's involvement in politics gave Soka Gakkai an image of intolerant militancy. Similar problems plagued many of the new religions that appeared in the United States in the last third of the twentieth century. Americans could tolerate a wide variety of religious beliefs, but those religions that stood out by adopting unfamiliar practices were subject to considerable public scrutiny. With controversy still plaguing the organization in Japan, SGI-USA attempted to avoid similar responses in America. Over time, considerations of legitimacy demanded that the American organization reform some of its practices to fit a very different social environment.

Perhaps the most noticeable changes were those designed to make Soka Gakkai accessible to English-speaking members. At first, meetings were conducted in Japanese, and the traditional practices of removing one's shoes before entering the room, kneeling on the floor before the Gohonzon, and sitting in sex-segregated groups were maintained in the American organization. As early as 1963, however, there were a sufficient number of English-speaking members to warrant the conduct of some meetings in English.[11] While the *gongyo* was still recited in Japanese, English transliterations of the Japanese characters were provided for English-speaking members. By the middle of the 1970s, participants were seated in folding chairs arranged in rows, and shoes remained on feet when American members entered the community center.

Although temples were built in the United States, the focus of SGI-USA activity is the community center, which bears limited signs of Japanese culture. These centers are often housed in rented business spaces, which, from the outside, are unlikely to be taken as places of religious activity. Even the decision what to call the organization in the United States seems to have been

---

[11] Hurst, "Nichiren Shoshu Soka Gakkai" (1980), 161.

motivated by a desire to avoid scrutiny. Hurst points out that the name originally chosen, Nichiren Shoshu of America, provided "an easy to pronounce acronym, NSA, which sounds very American."[12]

Similarly, the organizational structure of SGI in the United States was reformed to fit better into the American social environment. Imported as a pre-packaged whole, SGI-USA originally replicated the patriarchal form of the organization in Japan. Responding to criticisms by American members of the way authority was exercised, by the 1970s SGI-USA was turning its attention away from the national headquarters and toward local groups and community centers, adopting the congregational model of religious organization to which Americans are accustomed.[13] Similar criticisms of the undemocratic means of selecting leaders and exclusion of qualified women from positions of leadership led to reform. Today, the national organization is led by a legislative body representing the various regional groups, and women hold positions of leadership in rough proportion to their representation in the membership.

One result of this policy of Americanization is found in the changing ethnic makeup of SGI-USA leadership. Data on the ethnicity of leaders in the past are not available, but answers to a question in our 1997 survey asking whether these members have held leadership positions clearly suggest a pattern of change. Japanese respondents were more likely than others to say they *have held* national offices in the past (headquarters: 22 percent vs. 9 percent; area: 13 percent vs. 7 percent; and region: 10 percent vs. 2 percent). At present, Japanese and non-Japanese members hold such national offices in roughly equal proportion (headquarters: 7 percent vs. 9 percent; area: 7 percent vs. 3 percent; and region: 5 percent vs. 3 percent). However, Japanese members were *less* likely than others to say that they were *willing to hold* these offices in the future

---

[12] Ibid. 164.   [13] Ibid.

(headquarters: 10 percent vs. 26 percent; area: 13 percent vs. 25 percent; region: 12 percent vs. 27 percent). These findings not only demonstrate movement away from SGI-USA's heritage as an immigrant religion; they also suggest that the influence of Japanese members in the organization has declined and can be expected to decline further in the future. This shifting makeup of SGI-USA leadership will no doubt contribute to the continuing Americanization of the organization.

The same pattern may be observed in SGI's rhetoric. Soka Gakkai embraced American patriotism and materialism. Perhaps the clearest example of the former occurred around the time of the American bicentennial. Then, Soka Gakkai actively promoted American civil religion among its members. In 1976, for example, it held a tri-city convention in Boston, New York, and Phildelphia in conjunction with major bicentennial celebrations.[14] In speeches and literature, SGI leaders emphasized the continuities between the democratic ideal of a good society governed by an enlightened citizenship and the Buddhist goal of world peace through individual enlightenment.[15] Rhetorically, Soka Gakkai linked itself to American history, which the theme of SGI-USA's 1976 national convention clearly intimates: "Two hundred years from now."

Where other new religions of the 1960s decried American materialism, Soka Gakkai embraced it. To the communal religions of the period, for example, attachment to material goods only distracted people from their focus on higher goals, and led to selfishness and competitiveness. Soka Gakkai, alternatively, interpreted material success as evidence of the efficacy of the practice. Competitiveness and the achievement of specific, identifiable goals were portrayed as evidence of human revolution taking place in the individual's life. Instead of tuning in, turning on, and dropping out, Soka Gakkai members got focused, dove in, and got on with life.

---

[14] Hurst, "Nichiren Shoshu Soka Gakkai" (1980), 164; Metraux, *History and Theology of Soka Gakkai.*

[15] Hurst, "Nichiren Shoshu Soka Gakkai", 297–304.

The general tactic, in other words, has been one of accommodation to American culture. That this was a conscious tactic is evidenced in statements made by SGI leaders to earlier researchers. One regional director, in an interview with Daniel Metraux, for instance, says, "We can see what happens to other non-western religions when they get too much public attention."[16] Learning from the example of some other new religions that appeared on the scene after 1960, coupled with the experiences of the organization in Japan, Soka Gakkai took a low-profile stance. More neutral publicity campaigns such as sponsoring art and cultural exhibits, local performances, and subscription drives for SGI publications took the place of high-visibility practices such as parades and national conventions. Through these changes, Soka Gakkai courted a positive public image as it worked to develop its niche in the United States.

Without a doubt, this tactic cost the Soka Gakkai in terms of immediate utility. The more aggressive, high-visibility tactics used earlier in the organization's history correspond with periods of more rapid growth. As we saw in Chapter 2, the most rapid growth in SGI-USA took place from 1968 to 1975. During this time, Soka Gakkai grew at an average rate of 30 percent, or 3,085 persons, per year. For the remainder of the 1970s and the first two years of the 1980s, after SGI had adopted a policy of low-profile assimilation, the organization experienced a net loss of membership. A recovery in growth rates occurred during the 1980s, but it should be kept in mind that, in addition to renewed recruitment efforts, SGI was conducting a subscription drive among its members during this period, both for additional publicity and in order to bring in revenue. It was also a period of expanding Japanese corporate operations in the USA, which increased the number of immigrants from Japan, some of whom no doubt were (or became) SGI members. That apparent recovery, therefore, may not entirely reflect growth through

---

[16] Metraux, *History and Theology of Soka Gakkai*, 107–8.

conversion. Moreover, during the period of the schism (1990–1), SGI again experienced attrition—at a rate of about 15 percent per year. Membership since then has appeared to stabilize.

By opting to accommodate the institutions of American religion, then, and adopting a low-visibility approach to public relations, Soka Gakkai made sacrifices in terms of numerical growth. However, what Soka Gakkai sacrificed in short-term utility, it gained in legitimacy and thus acceptability.

The legitimacy SGI-USA attained is evidenced by the demographic profile of converts. The potential "cost" of membership in a "deviant" religion can be high, especially for white-collar professionals. Soka Gakkai's legitimacy made conversion a more realistic alternative for Americans of relatively high status. While close to 60 percent of the converts who responded to the 1997 survey had experienced some negative reactions from family or friends because of their involvement in Soka Gakkai, most minimized the significance of these experiences. They reported that family or friends were skeptical at first, but came around when they saw the positive impact that involvement was having on these converts' lives. One female member in New York, for instance, reported: "When I first joined, my stepmother had huge problems with my becoming a Buddhist (thought it was a cult). Since then, her attitude has totally changed (through seeing my life change)." Another woman in Pennsylvania reported that at first "my friends mocked me—now they remind me to chant for them." Some even reported that friends or family, who were critical at first, eventually tried chanting themselves.

That SGI-USA has attracted such respectable members (as described in Chapter 2) has, in turn, probably further contributed to the perception of legitimacy. It has certainly contributed to the organization's appeal. While adopting such a low-profile stance may have cost SGI-USA in terms of numerical growth and publicity, therefore, this tactic largely accounts for the religion's staying power. Soka Gakkai simply never experienced the kind of public conflict that plagued other new religions entering the field at about the same time. It went quietly about the business of organizational development, while many of its competitors, who had adopted positions in direct opposition to American mainstream culture, were publicly attacked, found bursts of growth short-lived, and now struggle to survive in the USA.

Recruitment Methods

The tactic of pursuing legitimacy over utility is evident in the changing recruitment practices of SGI-USA. The 1997 survey allows a closer examination of the Americanization of these recruitment practices. While the aggressive recruitment technique known as *shakubuku* was practiced in the United States during the early years of organizational development, by the mid-1970s, SGI-USA was opting instead for the more passive, soft-sell method sometimes called *shoju*. The data on numerical growth suggest that the change to a less aggressive tactic resulted in lower rates of recruitment, and possibly even a net loss of members. Data suggest, however, that this apparent cost to SGI-USA has not been as great as it might appear.

The practice of approaching strangers in public places and coaxing them to visit a Soka Gakkai meeting may result in a large number of potential recruits, but the likelihood that they will eventually join SGI and continue in the practice is low. This technique was thus associated with high rates of recruitment, but also with low rates of conversion. Most of the people introduced to Soka Gakkai through this means stayed long enough to satisfy whatever curiosity they may have had about a religion that advertises itself as a means to happiness and success in this world—but then left. In fact, the apparent decline in membership following the change from *shakubuku* to *shoju* probably reflects the lagging effects of *shakubuku*, which brought many people into the religion who then dropped out.

Furthermore, it seems likely that people recruited off the street, at bus stops, or on park benches would be socially marginal. Snow suggests that these recruits were characteristically dislocated—structurally available for recruitment, in that they had no particular obligations that would prevent them from experimenting with an alternative religion.[17] However, structural availability does not guarantee the kinds of predisposition associated with conversion to Soka Gakkai. Rather structural availability must be complemented by structural proximity to the religion for conversion to occur. In other words, the social ties pulling the potential recruit into Soka Gakkai must be stronger than countervailing social forces. People who encounter the religion at a time in their lives when they are structurally available, but who lack personal relationships with SGI-USA members, may agree to attend a meeting out of curiosity, but they are unlikely to join. As a recruitment method, therefore, *shakubuku* does not appear to be very effective.

The recruitment method known as *shoju* shows more promise. *Shoju* involves following up on "warm contacts"—people with whom the SGI member has an established relationship. Members will attempt to stimulate interest in friends and family by sharing with them their own experiences in SGI. When these members are seen as happy and successful, and they attribute their happiness and success to their religious practice, interest will be stimulated in others. This seems to be the primary means by which those recruits who eventually convert to SGI come to the practice. The typical pattern is exposure to the religion through some pre-existing acquaintance who generates the interest of a potential recruit by sharing the impact of participation on the member's own life and then invites the potential recruit to a Soka Gakkai gathering. There, the recruit will be exposed to others giving testimony to the positive benefits they've experienced. Even at this point, the sales pitch is low-pressure. The recruits will be invited to try chanting for

---

[17] Snow, Shakubuku.

themselves and see if it works. If not, they haven't lost anything. But if they experience changes in their lives, then they have proof that chanting does work and thus have access to a means of taking control of their lives.

Given the amount of effort it takes to learn how to chant, it is reasonable to think that people who encounter the religion and decide to try it out would need some reason to believe that chanting can deliver on its promises. Although transliterated for the convenience of English-speaking members, the *gongyo* is still chanted in Japanese. And, as we have seen, the recitation takes about forty minutes to complete, even at a very rapid pace, and the prescribed practice requires chanting the *gongyo* twice daily. Learning to chant thus requires a considerable investment on the part of the newcomer. Those who encounter the religion without any prior knowledge of it, or without any reason to believe the claims that chanting can change one's life, would have little reason to invest the time and energy needed to learn how to chant.

Understandably, then, very few of the respondents to the 1997 survey reported that they first encountered Soka Gakkai by means of *shakubuku*. Eighty-four percent of the converts in the sample indicated that they had been introduced to Soka Gakkai by their spouse, a member of their family, a work colleague, a friend, or some other pre-existing acquaintance. Only 2 percent indicated that they had first learned about Soka Gakkai through some impersonal means, such as attending an SGI-sponsored exhibition or concert, or through SGI literature and publicity. Of the 14 percent who checked the "other" response to this question, over half described encounters that also reflect the importance of pre-existing social ties. One woman, for instance, encountered SGI through her "boyfriend's roommate," another by "the mother of a boy who played soccer with my son." Thus, less than 7 percent, of the converts in the sample had been "*shakubukued*" while "sitting on a park bench," "by two women in a diner," or by "people going door to door."

The process of conversion will be discussed in more detail in the Chapter 6. But it is significant to the argument made here that few of the active members in 1997 were *shakubukued*. What appears to be a sacrifice of utility in the shift from *shakubuku* to *shoju* as a means of recruitment, therefore, may not have actually cost Soka Gakkai much in terms of actual conversion rates. If anything, the less aggressive, more publicly acceptable recruitment method constitutes a more efficient use of human resources because time and energy are not wasted trying to sell the religion to people who are unlikely to buy it.

Uniqueness

Soka Gakkai came to the United States not as a peace movement but as a religion, and a religion that is very distinctive relative to the Protestant tradition dominating religious culture in the United States. At first this point seems to go without saying, and chances are no one in the Soka Gakkai ever thought about the possibility of marketing the religion otherwise. In its culture of origin, however, Soka Gakkai has been as much a reform movement as a religious movement. As noted at the outset of this book, Soka Gakkai was founded originally as an educational society, and it has focused as much, if not more, on peace activities, education, and political reform as it has on religion. Apart from its association with Nichiren Buddhism in Japan, there is no particular reason why Soka Gakkai in the United States could not have marketed itself as a peace movement, affiliating with existing religions in the United States rather than entering into competition with them.

The Soka Gakkai, for instance, could have marketed itself in ways that would have played down the religious nature of the movement, organizing as a "Value Creation Society" and attempting to affiliate with existing religious organizations in the United States as a parachurch movement, much as the Promise Keepers have. In fact, Soka Gakkai has moved increasingly in that direction, focusing on the development of affiliated organizations, such as the Boston Research Center for the Twenty-First Century, Soka University, and cultural perform-ances and exhibits, even while membership in the religion itself appears to be lagging in the United States.

Of course, it is impossible to predict how successful Soka Gakkai would have been in America had it taken this alternative path. But the decision to compete as a religion clearly influ-enced the development of the organization in America. As shown in Chapter 3, it is through involvement in SGI-USA that members become aware of and engaged in Soka Gakkai's efforts to promote art, culture, education, and world peace. In prac-tical terms, this means that Soka Gakkai members must first convince potential recruits of the truth and efficacy of Nichiren Buddhism before selling them on collective efforts at social reform. No doubt, this approach has influenced both the num-ber and the type of people who get involved in SGI-USA. If, instead of asking converts to Nichiren Buddhism to "convert" as well to Soka Gakkai's peace activities, SGI-USA had recruited religious converts from among people already involved in its various, affiliated, "secular" organizations, the membership and pattern of growth might have looked very different. If nothing else, this alternative pattern would have expanded the pool of potential recruits beyond the immediate family and friends of Soka Gakkai members.

This discussion is, however, based on a hypothetical situ-ation; Soka Gakkai entered the American religious market place as a competitor with other religious organizations. As a con-sequence, the people most likely to get involved are people who are open to religious alternatives. The impact of this approach will become clearer as we examine the values of converts in Chapter 5 and the pattern of recruitment and conversion to Soka Gakkai in the Chapter 6.

In Conclusion

Soka Gakkai organized in the United States at a propitious time for religions of Eastern origin. Although present in America from as early as the 1940s, Soka Gakkai, because of conditions largely beyond its control, would not have experienced the development and growth of an organization here, even had those members already in the United States decided to try. Laws that restricted immigration from Japan did inhibit growth until 1965, when American immigration policy changed. The new immigrants were more likely to be professional men and there-fore also more likely to be received into positions of leadership in the Soka Gakkai, modeled as the organization was on the patriarchal form of Soka Gakkai in Japan. These newcomers not only provided the necessary functionaries to run the fledgling organization; they also provided SGI-USA greater financial resources and access to a broader portion of the American reli-gious public.

This new receptivity in the United States to religions of Eastern origin grew out of what might be described as a cultural awakening. From the crisis of meaning that accompanied America's entry into world politics in the period of the great wars, coupled with the growing awareness of religious diversity among the people who populated the United States, there emerged not an awakening to a new consensus, but an awaken-ing to pluralism. As the position of sovereignty once held by the mainstream Protestant denominations gave way, space was cre-ated in American society for new alternatives.

Not all of the new alternatives appearing during this time were equally successful, however. American tolerance for reli-gious diversity had limits, and those religions that pressed the limits too far—for example, by rejecting capitalism, the nuclear family, or other institutions central to the American way of life—were perceived as threatening and potentially dangerous. The anti-cult movement organized deliberately to stifle these religions. Compared to many such religions, the Soka Gakkai played the market very well. It accommodated American religious and social institutions, embracing and reinterpreting them in light of Nichiren Buddhism.

While the less aggressive, low-profile stance may have cost SGI-USA in terms of visibility and a reduction in the number of people who would be exposed to the religion, it paid off in terms of legitimacy. While other new religions were targeted by the anti-cult movement, Soka Gakkai grew quietly on the sideline. It achieved organizational stability where others held precariously, if at all, to their position in the American religious market. Although numerical growth has been less impressive than it might have been had Soka Gakkai used more aggressive means of recruitment, the more passive approach was probably a more efficient use of Soka Gakkai resources. By recruiting primarily through "warm contacts," Soka Gakkai focused its recruitment energies on those who were most likely to take an interest and join.

All told, Soka Gakkai was well positioned on the field. It was close enough to the cultural center to avoid attack by religious nativists, but sufficiently removed from that center to maintain its unique identity. It was positioned therefore to receive those young Americans who were seeking alternatives, as the religious center fragmented and gave way. Thus was SGI "supplied" in America.

5

Values and Conversions: The Question of Demand

WHILE clearly significant, supply-side conditions do not alone account for patterns of religious change. Shifts in the demands made by the religious public are also an important part of the story. Though frequently treated in the literature on new religions, there remains debate over how best to understand the appeal of new religions, especially those of Eastern origin, to people raised in Western religious traditions.

In this chapter, we examine the appeal of Soka Gakkai Buddhism to American converts. In Chapter 2, we noted that Soka Gakkai members are overwhelmingly employed in professional occupations that require specialized knowledge—that is, the new class of information occupations created as the American economy shifted to one of an advanced industrial society. Here, we demonstrate that American converts to Soka Gakkai also participate in a culture shift associated with this economic change—the shift from a producer-oriented culture to a culture oriented to consumption. But SGI-USA converts are not just participants in the emerging consumer culture. They are a particular type of consumer, whose choices are informed by a concern for the impact of their behavior on others and by a value orientation that we call "transmodern."

The transmodern subculture is not a new development in the American public. Elements of it can be observed in the 19th century in such movements as transcendentalism and spiritualism, as well as in religions such as Christian Science and Seventh-day Adventism that share with Soka Gakkai an emphasis on the oneness of spirit and matter, healing the self as a means of healing society, and other characteristics that will be described in more detail below.[1] Recent evidence suggests, however, that the transmodern subculture may be growing in the United States, thus creating a greater demand for religions with Soka Gakkai's characteristics.[2]

It is impossible to determine, definitively, whether the values that characterize converts to SGI-USA are a cause or consequence of their involvement in the religion. We attempted to gather data that might have allowed such a determination by asking respondents whether their answers to a number of attitudinal questions in the survey were influenced by their involvement in Soka Gakkai. If so, we then asked how they would have responded to these issues before joining—a good idea that didn't work. Most of the respondents apparently found it difficult to say what their responses might have been five, ten, or fifteen years ago. Most, therefore, simply left this section blank. Those who did respond indicated either that their values had not changed much, or that their attitudes are the same but stronger now than before. This pattern would indicate that, as one might expect, conversion to Soka Gakkai is best understood as people acting on pre-existing values rather than undergoing a dramatic transformation of world-view. However, only 17 percent of the respondents answered this retrospective question, which is not a sufficient response from which to generalize. Nonetheless, it makes sense to think that Americans already possessing a certain value orientation who encounter Soka Gakkai would be more likely to convert than people for whom conversion to Soka Gakkai would require a dramatic change in their thinking. At the same time, it must be

[1] Marty, *Modern American Religion*, ii.
[2] Paul Ray, "The Emerging Culture," *American Demographics*, 19/2 (1997), 29–34, 56.

acknowledged that value-similarity is not the whole answer, since, as we shall see, there are committed SGI members who seem not to fit the dominant SGI value profile. Demand-side theory, like supply-side theory, is part of the story, therefore, but not all of it. Put another way, the evidence to be discussed in this chapter does not replace or negate the findings of the previous chapter regarding supply-side factors. Rather, it augments those findings and contributes to a more complete picture of conversion and commitment to SGI-USA.

Soka Gakkai and Consumerism

In the epilogue to their study of Soka Gakkai in the United Kingdom, Bryan Wilson and Karel Dobbelaere hypothesized that the appeal of Soka Gakkai to British converts could be understood in relation to the shift from the producer-oriented culture of early industrial society to the consumer-oriented culture of advanced industrial society.[3] Our data support this hypothesis.

A developing industrial society requires large pools of capital for investment in factories and business, as well as a dedicated, hard-working labor force to operate those factories and businesses. In *The Protestant Ethic and the Spirit of Capitalism*, Max Weber demonstrated that the ethics promoted by Calvinist Protestantism contributed to the development of capitalism in both ways.[4] Protestants felt compelled to work hard in this world, perceiving their labor as a calling to be performed for the glory of God. But their concern for salvation and election to grace also meant that they should not squander the fruits of their labor, spending only what was necessary to sustain themselves until Jesus returned to gather those who had been chosen. The combination of hard work and frugality resulted in the accumulation of wealth—wealth that a good Protestant steward would invest in profitable endeavors.

[3] Wilson and Dobbelaere, *Time to Chant*.
[4] Max Weber, *The Protestant Ethic and the Spirit of Capitalism*, trans. Talcott Parsons (Los Angeles: Roxbury, 1998).

Protestant religion, characterized by this particular kind of inner-worldly asceticism, thus provided a moral warrant for the development of capitalism and, hence, industrial society. Things, however, change. As industrialism and economic growth led to an increase in per capita wealth, the willingness of individuals to accept the restrictions placed on consumption by Calvinist Protestantism decayed. Weber remarked that, as John Wesley himself had noted, the "full economic effect of those great religious movements . . . generally came only after the peak of the purely religious enthusiasm was past."[5] The religious asceticism of the early Protestants resulted in wealth that would tempt later generations to enjoy the leisure and consume the products that this wealth made possible.

In the United States, where rapid economic growth was combined with this distinctively Protestant religious heritage, a new problem challenged Protestant restrictions on consumption. To be sure, this problem was slow to emerge and even slower to be recognized, but once the industrial, capitalist economy was developed and functioning, continued economic growth and stability depended increasingly on spending and consumption. In an industrial economy, the potential for growth depends upon the size and strength of the market. According to some economists, "a high wage economy allows those who create wealth to share in its enjoyment, but it also produces levels of demand *necessary to an economy that is expanding to higher levels of activity*."[6]

When money is being saved instead of being used to purchase and consume the products of industry, the economy can stagnate, causing the value of capital to decline, thus reducing the incentive to invest in productive enterprises. When this happens, businesses are forced to scale back production, which usually means cutting labor costs by reducing wages and laying off workers. The result, of course, is even less incentive for

[5] Ibid. 176.
[6] Don Slater, *Consumer Culture and Modernity* (Cambridge, Mass.: Basil Blackwell, 1997), 178; emphasis added.

consumers to spend and more incentive to save money, or, in brief, a stagnant market created by "structurally insufficient demand."[7] Such a situation, in fact, contributed to the economic crisis experienced in the United States during the Great Depression.[8] The economy of an advanced industrial society, therefore, requires consumption. More significantly for the analysis here, it requires a culture that provides moral sanction, and even religious meaning, to the gratification of personal desires.

Ronald Inglehart suggests that just such a culture is emerging.[9] In an international study of value change in advanced industrial society, Inglehart discovered that as the overall level of economic and physical security rises, people come increasingly to value such non-material goods as self-expression, personal freedom, and aesthetic satisfaction. As long as such basic necessities as food, shelter, and physical safety were scarce, people tended to give priority to economic and physical security. Inglehart developed an index to measure the degree to which people in a number of nations were committed to material versus non-material values. Those choosing non-material over material values on the index were labeled "post-materialists." This index was reproduced in the study of SGI members in both the United Kingdom and the United States.

The index is constructed from answers to three questions asking respondents to rank "the aims of this country for the next ten years." Each question offers four possible goals, two of which reflect concerns for economic and physical security, and two that reflect a desire for such things as aesthetic satisfaction, personal freedom, and self-expression. Respondents were asked to put a number "1" beside their first choice, and "2" beside their second choice. The response categories for each of the three questions were as follows:

---

[7] Ibid.
[8] Ibid. 178–9.
[9] Ronald Inglehart, *Culture Shift in Advanced Industrial Society* (Princeton: Princeton University Press, 1988).

1. What should be the aims of this country for the next ten years? Below are listed some goals to which some people give priority. Would you please say which one of these you yourself consider the most important? And which would be the second most important? (Write "1" next to your first choice, and write "2" next to your second choice.)

    (*a*) Maintaining a high level of economic growth.
    (*b*) Making sure the country has strong defense forces.
    (*c*) Seeing that people have more say in how things are done at their jobs and in their communities.
    (*d*) Trying to make our cities and countryside more beautiful.

2. If you had to choose, which of the things on the list below would you say is most important? Which would you consider second most important? (Write "1" next to your first choice, and write "2" next to your second choice.)

    (*a*) Maintaining order in the nation.
    (*b*) Giving people more say in important government decisions.
    (*c*) Fighting rising prices.
    (*d*) Protecting freedom of speech.

3. Here is another list. In your opinion, which one of these is most important? And what would be the next most important? (Write "1" next to your first choice, and write "2" next to your second choice.)

    (*a*) A stable economy.
    (*b*) Progress towards a less impersonal and more humane society.
    (*c*) Progress towards a society in which ideas count more than money.
    (*d*) The fight against crime.

The index is constructed by giving two points for a first choice and one point for a second choice if the respondent chose one of the post-materialist answers (*c* and *d* in the first question, *b* and *d* in the second, and *b* and *c* in the third). The responses were assigned a value of zero if the respondent chose an answer valuing economic or physical security. Adding the scores together results in an index with ten possible scores, ranging from 0 to 9, with 9 indicating the "pure post-materialist," and 0, the "pure materialist." The results for SGI members in both the United States and Great Britain are reported in Table 24. A "mixed materialist" or "mixed post-materialist" is someone whose responses were mixed, but leaned toward materialist answers or non-materialist answers, respectively.

Table 24 demonstrates that in both the United States and Great Britain, SGI members tend to choose non-material values over material ones. The largest percentage of respondents in both cases is found, in fact, in the "pure post-materialist" category. By comparison, in the British public, the responses are distributed evenly along the index, with a small concentration in the middle. A similar pattern is found when these responses are compared with those of the American public.

Our knowledge of the American public on this issue comes from the 1990 World Values Survey conducted by Gallup. The results are compelling. As in Great Britain, converts to SGI in the United States fall overwhelmingly in the post-materialist

Table 24. Post-materialism index (%)

Category	Public, United Kingdom[a]	SGI-UK[a]	Public, United States[b]	SGI-USA
Pure materialist (0–2)	21	2	36	7
Mixed materialist (3–4)	28	3	33	18
Mixed post-materialist (5–6)	30	20	20	30
Pure post-materialist (7–9)	21	75	11	45

Source: [a] Bryan Wilson and Karen Dobbelaere, *A Time to Chant* (Oxford: Clarnedon Press, 1994), 143. The British authors used scores of 1–10 rather than 0–9.

[b] 1990 World Values Survey. Data provided by Microcase Corporation.

camp, choosing self-expression and freedom over economic and physical security at nearly three times the rate of the public at large. SGI-USA members are four times more likely to be pure post-materialists than the American public. The probability of getting such large differences between the sample results for SGI converts and the public by chance is negligible.[10] Most SGI-USA converts can accurately be located in the post-materialist camp.

From these results, other kinds of expectation follow. For example, in a society where scarcity is the rule (whether actual, as in the case of poverty, or ethically imposed as in the case of Puritan America), individuals will rely more heavily on the group for personal security. In such a society, people can be expected to place more emphasis on family, which forms the most immediate source of economic and physical security. In a society characterized by relative affluence, by contrast, in which individuals rely less heavily on the family and demand more personal freedom and autonomy, it can be expected that they will place less emphasis on family life. In the United States, for instance, the trend is toward smaller families, started later in life. Marriages are delayed and more often end in divorce. Marriage, which under conditions of scarcity is a prescribed ritual for entry into adulthood required by economic necessity, tends to become simply an option oriented to personal fulfillment in a consumer-oriented culture.

The relatively low priority given to marriage and child-rearing by SGI-USA members further demonstrates, therefore, their consumer orientation (Table 25). SGI-USA members place significantly less emphasis on marriage and family life than do most Americans. In fact, SGI-USA members are less likely to

[10] For these and the following results, significance was evaluated using a one-tail test of difference in proportions between two samples. See Allan Johnson, *Statistics* (San Diego: Harcourt, Brace, Jovanovich, 1988): 336–9 for details. Since *N* for the GSS is very large, we accepted the null hypothesis if the probability that observed differences is zero was greater than 0.01. Unless otherwise noted, all of the results reported in this chapter are significant at $p < 0.01$ or less.

be married than respondents to the General Social Survey. That SGI-USA members think of marriage as a self-expressive act oriented to personal fulfillment is further evidenced by the large proportion who have been divorced. Compared to 23 percent of respondents to the GSS, 44 percent of SGI-USA members have experienced a divorce. Based on these data, then, it can safely be said that converts to SGI-USA have an identifiably "consumerist" attitude towards marriage and family life.

Table 25. Importance of marriage and family to SGI-USA members (%)

Indicators	SGI-USA	GSS, age adjusted
Assessed as "very important":		
Being married	38	50
Having kids	48	62
Current marital status:		
Married	38	48
Living with a partner	8	n.a.
Has been divorced	44	23
N^a	315	1,584

Note: Questions 51, 96, and 97 in the questionnaire, App. C.
n.a. = not available.

  [a] *N* varies.

Source: The source for the last column is General Social Survey (GSS), 1993, 1996.

Hammond has argued that the greater individual freedom experienced by people living in the United States today is associated with a shift in emphasis from "collective-expressive" roles based on ascribed traits (such as gender, family, and ethnicity) to "individual-expressive" roles based on achieved traits (such as education or skill).[11] In addition to religious behavior, which was Hammond's main concern in exploring this shift, two other areas in which this shift has been most profound are gender

---

[11] Hammond, *Religion and Personal Autonomy*.

roles and sexuality. Here, too, we can observe the consumer orientation of SGI-USA converts.

Under conditions of relative scarcity, roles expressive of the needs and expectations of the group take precedence over self-expressive pursuits. For women, this typically meant confinement to the domestic realm and the roles of wife, mother, and keeper of the home. The greater individual autonomy and declining emphasis on marriage and family life in contemporary American society have resulted in a greater demand by women to pursue their ambitions outside of the home. As already noted in Chapter 2, female converts to SGI-USA are only half as likely as their counterparts in the American public to be full-time homemakers. They are considerably more likely to be employed in a full-time occupation. We see now that the attitudes of these women converts about traditional gender roles also differ dramatically (Table 26). Women in SGI-USA are much less likely than their peers in the American public to accept the roles traditionally ascribed to women.

Related to these changes in attitudes about marriage and gender are changes in the meaning of sex. The Protestant habit

Table 26. Women's attitudes about gender roles (% agree)

Statement	SGI-USA	GSS, age adjusted
All in all, family life suffers when the woman has a full-time job	21	34
A job is alright, but what most women really want is a home and children	12	30
A husband's job is to earn money; a wife's job is to look after the home and family	9	23
N^a	203	813

Note: Question 54 in the questionnaire, App. C.

  [a] *N* varies.

Source: The source for the last column is General Social Survey (GSS), 1994.

of self-restraint translated into many restrictions on sexual pleasure. Sexuality was to be carefully controlled and oriented to procreation. Sexuality in the consumerist mind, by contrast, is a means of emotional expression and personal gratification. Consumerists tend, therefore, to reject many traditional sexual taboos. Not surprisingly, the attitudes about sexuality held by Soka Gakkai members fall clearly in the consumerist camp (Table 27). Though sizeable majorities of both the American public and SGI converts reject teenage sex and extra-marital sex, the SGI members are less rejecting when it comes to sex before marriage and homosexuality. SGI converts are only one third as likely as the American public to disapprove of these behaviors (10 percent vs. 32 percent, and 20 percent vs. 65 percent).

Table 27. Attitudes about sexuality (% "always" or "almost always" wrong)

Sexual behavior	SGI-USA	GSS, age adjusted
Sex before marriage	10	32
Teenagers having sex	76	86
Extra-marital sex	82	93
Homosexuality	20	65
N	310	1,876

Note: Question 76 in the questionnaire, App. C.

Source: The source for the last column is General Social Survey (GSS), 1996.

The moral latitude Soka Gakkai members give to others is further reflected in their attitudes toward abortion and marijuana. Converts to SGI are considerably more likely than the American public to approve of legal abortion. Seventy-three percent of SGI-USA converts said that a woman should be able to get a legal abortion if she is married and does not want more children, compared to 48 percent of GSS respondents. Converts were also more likely to say a woman should be able to get an abortion if the family is poor (75 percent vs. 47 percent), if the woman is single and does not want to marry the father (69 percent vs. 46 percent), indeed, if she wants it for any reason (67 percent vs. 46 percent). Results were similar on the topic of marijuana. Converts were twice as likely to say that marijuana should be legal (58 percent vs. 28 percent of GSS respondents).

Such a libertarian attitude toward individual moral behavior requires optimism about people. That is, to grant others considerable moral latitude requires a belief that, given the opportunity to make their own decisions, people will choose the good. In fact, converts to SGI-USA, relative to the American public, are very optimistic about people. Three indicators commonly used to measure optimism versus despair illustrate the point (Table 28). The majority of converts to SGI-USA say they believe that, in general, people try to be helpful, fair, and trustworthy. The chances of finding this kind of optimism in the American public are fifty-fifty at best, whereas among SGI converts, the proportion is closer to two thirds. Soka Gakkai members, therefore, not only believe that people should be given considerable freedom to make moral decisions, but they are also more likely to believe that people are worthy of this kind of liberty.

These findings support the Wilson and Dobbelaere hypothesis that Soka Gakkai has a message with "special relevance" for people living in the "climate of economic and social

Table 28. Optimism (% agree)

Attitude	SGI-USA	GSS, age adjusted
People try to be helpful	68	43
People try to be fair	62	50
Most people can be trusted	52	35
N	320	1,905

Note: Questions 56–8 in the questionnaire, App. C.

Source: The source for the last column is General Social Survey (GSS), 1996.

permissiveness" characterizing advanced industrial society.[12] Soka Gakkai Buddhism, by interpreting personal happiness, success, and material well-being as evidence of the process of spiritual transformation, gives religious meaning and moral sanction to self-gratification and the enjoyment of life. Just as the Protestant ethic of hard work, thrift, and duty was suited to a producer-oriented culture, so the Buddhist ethic promoted by Soka Gakkai is suited to a culture in which the pursuit of pleasure, consumption, and individual autonomy is increasing.

SGI-USA's approval of self-gratification and individual freedom is not, however, without a broader social ethic. The pursuit of individual satisfaction in life is encompassed by a concern for the well-being of the whole. Soka Gakkai promotes its brand of Buddhism not only as a means to personal happiness, but ultimately as a means to world peace. Soka Gakkai advances a soteriological vision of a world without nuclear weapons, war, poverty, and crime. While characterized by an almost libertarian perspective on individual behavior, Soka Gakkai converts are also driven by an ascetic impulse oriented to social reform. Let us explore this issue.

Global Citizens

To describe Soka Gakkai members as "ascetic" is admittedly stretching the meaning of the term, which is most commonly associated with the strict personal discipline of monasticism. But through the conception of the "calling," Protestants brought asceticism into the mundane world of daily labor. It was this rigorous self-discipline, Weber argued, that contributed so greatly to the rise of capitalism. We have said converts to SGI-USA infuse immediate self-gratification with religious meaning and moral sanction. In what sense, then, can they be described as "ascetic"?

---

[12] Wilson and Dobbelaere, *Time to Chant*, 220.

The asceticism of converts to SGI-USA is aptly captured in the phrase "Think globally. Act locally." Soka Gakkai members, while libertarian in their attitudes toward personal morality, are made conscious of the fact that their own behavior has consequences for the environment, their community, their society, and ultimately the world. This commitment to contribute to the development of a more beautiful and harmonious world is evident in these converts' attitudes about science and technology, the environment, and poverty. We examine these attitudes now.

Converts to SGI-USA are no more critical of science and technology than the average American. When asked, for instance, whether science does more harm than good, the responses of SGI-USA members are virtually identical to those of GSS respondents (14 percent and 15 percent agreeing, respectively). Differences emerge, however, when asked if people worry too much about human progress harming the environment. More than a third of the American public think so (35 percent), but only half that percentage of converts do (18 percent). This kind of asceticism emerges again in response to another question about the environment. Only 8 percent of converts agree that it is "too difficult for someone like me to do much about the environment," compared to 26 percent of GSS respondents. And converts are more likely to agree with the statement, "I do what is right for the environment, even when it costs more money or takes up more time" (69 percent vs. 54 percent, $p < 0.00$).

The combination of personal freedom and social responsibility is reflected, as well, in the answers converts gave to two questions that can be regarded as indicators of altruism. Respondents were asked how strongly they agreed or disagreed with each of the following statements:

You have to take care of yourself first, and if you have any energy left over, then help other people.

People should be allowed to accumulate as much wealth as they can even if some make millions while others live in poverty.

Converts to SGI-USA were more likely than the American public to agree with the first statement, but less likely to agree with the second (Table 30). On the surface, these results appear contradictory. However, in light of the asceticism described above, the pattern makes sense. Converts to Soka Gakkai place a high value on taking responsibility for one's own life, but also for the impact of one's behavior on other people. The first statement, which reflects a concern for others, is more consistent with this attitude than the second, which reflects a desire for self-gratification without a concern for the impact of one's actions on other people.

Table 29. Altruism (% "agree" or "agree strongly")

Attitude	SGI-USA	GSS, age adjusted
Take care of yourself first	54	45
People should be allowed to accumulate wealth	38	58
N[a]	315	1,502

Note: Question 63 in the questionnaire, App. C.

[a] *N* varies.

Source: "Take care of yourself first": General Social Survey (GSS), 1996; "People should be allowed to accumulate wealth": GSS 1993.

Perhaps the most telling indicator of the ascetic conscience of converts is the pattern of responses to four questions about the causes of poverty. Respondents were asked why some people in this country live in need. Four possible reasons for poverty were given, and respondents were asked to rate each as "very important," "somewhat important," or "not important." Two of the explanations for poverty located the cause in individual behavior: (1) loose morals and drunkenness, and (2) lack of effort by the poor themselves. Two other explanations attributed poverty to flaws in the social system: (1) failure of society to provide good schools for many Americans, and (2) failure of industry to provide enough jobs. Responses to these four questions were assigned a value of 0 if the respondents chose "not import-ant," 1 if they chose "somewhat important," and 2 if they chose "very important." These four variables can therefore be com-bined into two indexes—one measuring the degree to which respondents attribute poverty to individual behavior (question 1 + question 2), and the other measuring the degree to which respondents attribute poverty to flaws in the social system (question 3 + question 4). Scores on both indexes range from 0 to 4. By cross-tabulating the two indexes, we achieve a table that can be summarized in four cells (Figure 2).

Figure 2. Response patterns to the question "Why are there people in this country who live in need?"

[Attributes poverty to social causes]

Attributes poverty to individual behaviour	No (0–2)	Yes (3–4)
No (0–2)	Fatalist	Liberal
Yes (3–4)	Conservative	Transmodern

The responses most common in the American public might be described as "fatalist." That is, this group attributes poverty neither to individuals as moral actors nor to problems in the social system. To them, poverty just "is." Thirty-one percent of GSS respondents, but only 21 percent of converts, chose this response (Table 30). By comparison, the most frequent response among SGI converts implicated both individual behavior and the social system (35 percent; in Figure 2, the "transmodern" response). This response pattern is found less often in the public at large (24 percent). Foreshadowing our conclusion to this chapter, we have termed this response pattern "transmodern," because persons giving this response under-stand that problems in the social system contribute to poverty,

Table 30. Causes of poverty (%)

Category	SGI-USA	GSS, age adjusted
Transmodern	35	24
Conservative	15	27
Liberal	29	19
Fatalist	21	31
N	304	1,275

Note: Question 55 in the questionnaire, App. C.

Source: The source for the last column is General Social Survey (GSS), 1990.

but they also believe that responsibility falls on individuals to overcome these challenges.

The second most common response among converts corresponds to the position of the political left. According to this "liberal" position, if human beings naturally tend toward the good, then social problems such as crime and poverty must exist because of flaws in the social system, and the remedy lies in reforming the system through government intervention. SGI converts are least likely to give the "conservative" response that reflects what has been described as the "new economic orthodoxy" of the political right.[13] According to this viewpoint, society is the cumulative effect of choices made by individuals. Poverty, therefore, results when individuals make poor decisions, and the body politic is not collectively accountable.

Here again we observe the unique style of asceticism that characterizes converts to Soka Gakkai. It is an asceticism that disciplines the social, rather than the physical, body. While converts value their personal freedom and enjoy considerable autonomy in making individual moral decisions, they also exhibit a strong concern for the impact of their own behavior on other people and on the environment. In this way, therefore, the value orientation of converts differs from simple libertarian-

---

[13] Bill Jordan, *The Common Good: Citizenship, Morality, and Self-Interest* (New York: Basil Blackwell, 1987).

ism. Whereas the libertarian position promotes a society in which individuals are free to do what they will, unencumbered by social restraint, the "transmodern" ethic promotes a society of individuals free to make moral decisions but responsible as well for the impact of their decisions on others.

Soka Gakkai and Transmodernism

As we stated at the beginning of this chapter, transmodern religiosity has a history in American culture, recognizable since the nineteenth century. Religions such as Christian Science, Seventh-day Adventism, and later neo-orthodox Protestantism sought to recover a sense of wholeness in response to the way that modernity "chopped up aspects of life which once . . . had been held together."[14] Put another way, transmodernism sought to bring together the best of modernity and the inherited wisdom of religious traditions. In this section, we show how transmodernism differs from other religious responses to modernity, and demonstrate that the values of SGI-USA converts locate them clearly in the transmodern camp.

Religious persons in America have taken one of four positions in response to modernity. At the extremes of the spectrum are those who reject religion as superstition in favor of science and reason (modernism), and those who reject modernity on the basis of traditional religious convictions (counter-modernism). In between are those who accept scientific methods and even use them to enhance religious understanding, a viewpoint associated with the liberal Protestant tradition. Also in between, however, are those who accept the wisdom of religious traditions but use that wisdom for guidance in social and scientific "progress."[15] It is this fourth—"transmodern"—response that best characterizes the religious thinking of converts to Soka Gakkai.

As the prefix "trans" suggests, transmodern culture is concerned with going beyond modernity.[16] This implies that

14 Marty, *Modern American Religion*, i. 251.
15 Ibid.   16 Ibid.

modernity has its limits—limits that have been dramatically displayed by the destructive potential of technology, war, economic crisis, and the persistence of human problems such as crime, disease, and poverty. While transmodernism possesses an overall optimism about the possibility of human development through knowledge—one of the key characteristics of modernity—transmoderns are wary of the idea of progress. They tend to question whether progress is always an improvement. Knowledge without the wisdom to use it can be dangerous; technology, almost always billed as improving the conditions of human life, used carelessly can result in problems greater than those the technology was designed to solve. For instance, drug-resistant strains of certain viruses develop because of uncritical use of powerful antibiotics.

Out of such criticisms comes an emphasis on the limitations of the human condition and, consequently, a certain humility in the face of realities beyond human understanding. In neo-orthodox Protestantism, for example, there is the renewed emphasis on original sin. In many traditions, there is recognition of human dependence on the environment that takes the form of a view of nature as sacred, as well as a sense of human interconnectedness manifested in an appreciation for human diversity.

Related to this sense of humility is an emphasis on healing and wholeness. The therapeutic orientation of transmodern culture is evident in groups such as The Forum seminar training (formerly Erhard's Seminar Training (*est*), Scientology, Transcendental Meditation, and A Course in Miracles, as well as in the writing of popular "new age" authors, such as Deepak Chopra and Louis Haye. In these cases, the boundaries between secular psychotherapy and religion are blurred. These movements are also concerned with healing the physical body, reclaiming the body as intrinsically sacred as opposed to the "earthen vessel" of the spirit. Furthermore, these movements are tied together by the belief in healing the individual as a means of healing society.

A further characteristic of transmodernism is a fascination with the exotic. In part, this interest in foreign culture is a man-

ifestation of the transmodern sense of human interconnectedness, but it also reflects the fact that transmodernism seeks
alternatives to traditional Western ways of perceiving the world.

Transmodernism thus denies the classic Western dualisms
that set spirit apart from matter, self apart from other, male
apart from female, and culture apart from nature. The popularity of books on sacred sexuality, for example, is evidence of the
expansion of transmodern thought in American culture, as are
retreats, seminars, and books on discovering and expressing the
self through art, meditation, and ritual.

This trend has even captured the attention of market demo-
graphers, who recognize in transmodernism a novel kind of
consumer. Paul Ray, for instance, estimates that as many as 44
million American adults (24 percent of the adult US population) fit the transmodern profile.[17] Demographically, Ray's
description of transmodernists matches the *demography* of
converts to SGI-USA to near perfection. Women are over-
represented in both groups by a 60:40 ratio.[18] Both groups are
predominantly composed of highly educated Baby Boomers
employed in white-collar occupations. And, it turns out,
American converts to Soka Gakkai also possess many of the *values* that, according to Paul Ray, typify the transmodern subculture.

The concern of SGI-USA converts for the environment has
already been demonstrated above. But what distinguishes the
transmodern view of nature is the belief that nature is sacred.
When asked about their views of nature, converts to SGI-USA
are three times more likely than the American public to say that
they perceive nature as "spiritual or sacred in itself" (Table 31).
Given their non-theistic religious beliefs, it is not surprising that
only four SGI-USA converts chose the response that describes
nature as God's creation. However, even adding in the 38 percent of the public who view nature as sacred "because it is created by God," the converts are twenty percentage points more

---

[17] Ray, "The Emerging Culture," 29.   [18] Ibid. 30.

Table 31. View of nature (%)

Response	SGI-USA	GSS, age adjusted
Nature is sacred because it is created by God	1	38
Nature is spiritual or sacred in itself	81	24
Nature is important, but not spiritual or sacred	17	39
N	296	1,209

Note: Question 64 in the questionnaire, App. C.

Source: The source for the last column is General Social Survey (GSS), 1994.

likely than the American public to view nature as sacred. Converts were less than half as likely as the GSS respondents to say that nature is just nature, neither spiritual nor sacred.

American converts to a religion of Eastern origin obviously have an interest in exotic culture. By definition, therefore, converts to SGI satisfy the xenophilia that Ray says characterizes transmodernism. In the next chapter we suggest that this interest in Asian culture preceded conversion to Soka Gakkai. This appreciation for human diversity is further evidenced by converts' attitudes toward immigrants and ethnic minorities (Table 32). Although converts were only slightly more likely than the public to think that increased immigration would lead to higher economic growth ($p < 0.05$), they were significantly *less* likely to expect negative consequences of immigration, such as unemployment or disunity ($p < 0.00$). And converts were twice as likely to say that the experiences of racial and ethnic minorities do not receive adequate attention in high school and college classes.

Ray further claims that transmoderns are "consumers of culture," more so than other groups in the American public. In particular, they are consumers of those cultural products associated with self-improvement, such as experiential retreats—a

Table 32. Attitudes toward immigrants (%)

Attitude	SGI-USA	GSS, age adjusted
Increased immigration will "very likely" lead to:		
Higher economic growth	15	9
Higher unemployment	32	56
Making it harder to keep the country united	11	35
The experiences of racial and ethnic minorities receive "too little attention" in history classes taught in high school and college	54	25
N	313	1,352

Note: Questions 80–1 in the questionnaire, App. C.

Source: The source for the last column is General Social Survey (GSS), 1994.

pattern consistent with what has so far been discovered about SGI converts. The similarity goes much further, however. Ray indicates that transmoderns "buy more books and magazines than average. They also listen to more radio, especially classical music and public radio, and watch less television than the other groups."[19] Transmoderns, furthermore, are found to be "more likely than the average American to be involved in the arts as amateurs or pros, to write books and articles, and to go to cultural meetings and workshops."[20] This description could just as well have been written of converts to SGI-USA (Table 34). SGI-USA converts spend more time engaged in artistic pursuits and are more likely to be involved in small groups reflecting such interests than the American public. They spend less time than the average American watching television.

Despite their caution about the impact of science and technology on the environment and their awareness of the limitations of the human condition, transmoderns are generally optimistic

[19] Ibid. 32.   [20] Ibid.

Table 33. Cultural consumption (%)

Cultural activities	SGI-USA	GSS, age adjusted
(1) Activities in the last year		
Visited art museum or gallery	75	42
Made art or craft objects, such as pottery, woodworking, quilts, or paintings	51	40
Gone to a live ballet or dance performance	47	20
Gone to a classical music or opera performance	37	16
Taken part in a music, dance, or theatrical performance	30	10
Played a musical instrument such as a piano, guitar or violin	29	24
N	312	1,592
(2) Membership in nationality or ethnicity groups	14	5
Membership in literary, art, discussion, or study groups	33	11
N	311	1,558
(3) Average hours spent watching television every day	2.19	2.88
N	306	1,947

Note: Questions 48 and 50 in the questionnaire, App. C.

Sources: For (1): General Social Survey (GSS), 1993; for (2): GSS 1994; for (3): GSS 1996.

about the future. As with the pattern of cultural consumption, Ray's description of transmoderns in this regard might have been taken directly from a Soka Gakkai publication. Ray writes: "they believe that rebuilding and healing society is related to healing the self, physically and spiritually. With that goes a guarded social optimism."[21] The optimism of converts has been demonstrated in their attitudes toward other people, but two additional indicators demonstrate that this optimism extends to the social world. Respondents were asked whether they agreed or disagreed with each of the statements in Table 34. The optimism of converts to SGI-USA relative to the American public is marked. Converts were more likely to disagree with the idea that the "situation of the average person is getting worse," and to disagree that "it is not fair to bring a child into the world" given the condition ours is in.

Table 34. Social optimism (% disagree)

Attitude	SGI-USA	GSS, age adjusted
In spite of what some people say, the lot (situation/condition) of the average person is getting worse, not better	52	31
It's hardly fair to bring a child into the world with the way things look for the future	69	56
N	315	1,221

Note: Question 72 in the questionnaire, App. C.
Source: The source for the last column is General Social Survey (GSS), 1994.

As indicators of transmodernism, these questions are convincing but admittedly less than perfect. One reason for this imperfection stems from the fact that they were selected from the General Social Survey (GSS) as the best available questions asked of the American public. Using questions from the GSS made it possible to compare the values of SGI-USA converts with those held by the American public, thus allowing us to evaluate statistically the notion that conversion to SGI is related

---

[21] Ibid.

to the transmodern subculture. If that relationship could be shown, it would be critical support for the "demand" side of our argument. Because the General Social Survey represents the best and most accessible source of data on American public opinion, it therefore can be used as a control group for evaluating similarities and differences between any particular population and the American public generally—an exercise too often neglected in studies of new religions.[22]

This method, however, is subject to certain limitations. In order to be strictly comparable, the questions in both surveys must be identical. Changes in the wording of questions or response categories render statistical comparisons suspect. This means that, although different questions, or questions worded differently, might have captured better the phenomenon described here as transmodernism, for comparison purposes we had to use the best indicators available in the GSS.

Despite this limitation, however, the data just reviewed provide powerful support for the hypothesized relationship between transmodernism and conversion to Soka Gakkai. This relationship suggests, therefore, a demand in the American public for religions with characteristics like those of the Soka Gakkai.

Comparison with SGI-UK

Because an American control group was needed for testing the transmodernism hypothesis, questions drawn from the General Social Survey took precedence over questions asked in the survey of SGI members in Great Britain, placing certain limitations on the comparability of the two studies. Many questions from the SGI-UK survey were included in the SGI-USA survey, however.[23] Therefore, it is possible to evaluate to a limited degree

[22] See Robbins, *Cults, Converts, and Charisma*, 14–17 for a critical evaluation of method in studies of new religions.
[23] Since the SGI-UK study surveyed only converts, data from the SGI-USA survey in this section are limited to converts as well.

whether the findings reported here also apply to SGI members in Great Britain.

Wilson and Dobbelaere, for example, report that SGI members in Great Britain are more flexible in their attitudes about sexuality than is the case for the British public. We have already observed that the same holds true in the United States. But how do British and American converts compare? Both surveys included a question about sexual freedom; respondents were asked whether individuals should be able to "enjoy complete sexual freedom without being restricted." American members were slightly more conservative in their responses to this question than their British peers (Table 35). In both cases, however, the modal response was "it depends," reflecting a situational ethic—a position that hardly registered (10 percent) in the British public. SGI members in both countries, it seems safe to say, are relatively tolerant of a diversity of sexual behaviors, but they do not go so far as to say that there are no rights and wrongs where sexuality is concerned.

Wilson and Dobbelaere interpret this pattern to mean that for SGI-UK members sexuality is a matter of personal responsibility rather than public concern. This interpretation is bolstered by SGI-UK members' responses to a question asking

Table 35. Should there be complete, unrestricted sexual freedom? (%)

Reply	SGI-USA	SGI-UK	UK, age adjusted
Tend to agree	23	25	32
Tend to disagree	34	24	57
Neither, it depends	43	49	10
No answer	1	2	1
N	310	619	—

Note: Question 77 in the questionnaire, App. C.

Source: The source for the last two columns is Bryan Wilson and Karer Dobbelaere, *Time to Chant* (Oxford: Clarendon Press, 1994), 129.

whether it is proper for religious bodies to speak out on such issues as homosexuality, extra-marital affairs, abortion, and euthanasia. In Great Britain, converts tend to think it is *not* proper for religious bodies to make pronouncements on such issues. Wilson and Dobbelaere are probably correct in thinking that this question was taken by respondents to mean "should religious bodies speak out *against*" these behaviors, and, having no objection themselves to such behavior, were less willing to grant other religious bodies the privilege of speaking out. The same assumptions probably hold true in the case of respondents to the SGI-USA survey. Nevertheless, American Soka Gakkai members were more likely to perceive these issues as appropriate subjects of religious debate (Table 36). Because of the ambiguity involved in the question's wording, however, any interpretation of this set of findings must remain speculative.

SGI-USA members' answers to a related set of questions lend some possible clarification of the situation. We have already seen that SGI members are more likely than the British public to adopt a situational ethic. On the basis of two questions asked of American members (but not of British members), we learn that SGI-USA members are *less* likely than the American public to say that immoral acts by one person can corrupt all of society

Table 36. Is it proper for religious bodies to speak out on issues related to the family? (% agree)

Issue	SGI-USA	SGI-UK	UK, age adjusted
Homosexuality	51	35	51
Extra-marital affairs	52	35	54
Abortion	52	48	58
Euthanasia	59	55	64
N	310	619	n.a.

Note: Question 49 in the questionnaire, App. C.
n.a. = not available.

Source: The source for the last two columns is Bryan Wilson and Karel Dobbelaere, *Time to Chant* (Oxford: Clarendon Press, 1994), 132.

Table 37. Moral absolutism (% "agree" or "agree strongly")

Moral viewpoint	SGI-USA converts	SGI-USA non-converts	GSS, age adjusted
Right and wrong are not usually a simple matter of black and white; there are many shades of gray	91	93	86
Immoral actions by one person can corrupt society in general.	61	66	74
Morality is a personal matter and society should not force everyone to follow one standard	66	66	51
N	318	74	1,430

Note: Question 75 in the questionnaire, App. C.

Source: The source for the last column is General Social Survey (GSS), 1988.

(Table 37). And they are *more* likely than the American public to say that morality is a personal matter. This finding holds for SGI-USA members who were born into SGI, or switched to SGI from some other Asian religion. It must be noted, however, that the differences between SGI-USA members and the American public, while statistically significant, are not dramatic. This finding is consistent, therefore, with Wilson and Dobbelaere's generalization about SGI members, though it suggests one way that SGI-USA members remain "typically American."

The differences between American and British SGI members might well reflect a particular feature of American religion. Tocqueville noted in the 1830s that, while in America the separation of church and state was nearly complete, preachers in America never stood down from the opportunity to apply religious principles to mundane concerns. The pervasive and lasting impact of religion on public morality made religion, for Tocqueville, "the first of their political institutions, for although it did not give them the taste for liberty, it singularly facilitates their use thereof."[24] Americans are in the habit of thinking about religion and morality as matters of public concern and may be more likely than people of other Western countries to accept the legitimacy of public pronouncements by religious bodies on controversial issues, even when they disagree with the substance of those pronouncements. SGI members in the United States—converts and non-converts alike—apparently, cannot escape entirely their cultural environment.

On other indicators, differences between SGI members in the United States and Great Britain are less telling. American members are *less* likely than their British counterparts to say that it would be a good thing if people de-emphasized money and material possessions (67 percent vs. 86 percent). They are only half as likely to say that a "decrease in the importance of work in our lives" would be a good thing (17 percent vs. 28 percent). And American members appear to place less emphasis than their British counterparts on having leisure time. We cannot answer definitively why this should be the case, but chances are these results are related to the different occupational profiles of the two groups. As noted earlier, SGI members in Great Britain are more likely to be self-employed and to be employed as artists or artisans than American members. The differences in attitudes toward work and leisure may be a function therefore of different positions of the two groups in the labor force. American members are more likely to be employed in competitive professional and corporate occupations, and are probably, therefore, more likely to be immersed in a success ethic.

SGI members in both countries are involved in a variety of voluntary associations and altruistic activities. Even given their existing time commitments—to work and to SGI—these members make time to be involved in what they regard as good

---

[24] Alexis de Tocqueville, *Democracy in America*, trans. G. Lawrence (Garden City, NY: Anchor Books, 1969), 292.

causes. This provides some evidence, therefore, that the kind of asceticism found among SGI converts in the United States is probably also to be found among converts in Great Britain.

In summary, the minor differences that emerge between SGI members in the United States and Great Britain do not change the overall conclusion that conversion to Soka Gakkai is, in part, a function of the value orientation described here as transmodern. In both countries, the values of converts reflect what Wilson and Dobbelaere describe as a consumer orientation. In both cases, the individualism reflected in matters of personal morality is balanced by an altruistic concern for the social body. In both cases, involvement in SGI brings converts into contact with other people who, for the most part, share their perspective on the world.

The Appeal of Soka Gakkai

Converts to SGI-USA hold social values that tend to set them apart from others in the American public. While it is impossible, given the limitations of the data, to establish that these converts held such values prior to conversion, there is reason to believe that most converts were moving in this direction when they encountered Soka Gakkai. It is noteworthy, for instance, that many of those converts who engaged in a pattern of religious exploration prior to joining SGI had been involved in religions that, like SGI, can be described as transmodern in orientation. Such religions include Christian Science, Mind Science, Transcendental Meditation, Unitarianism, Unity, and the Self-Realization Fellowship. If this subcultural perspective were unique to Soka Gakkai members, we would be inclined to think that these transmodern values result from resocialization into a new religion. However, this subcultural orientation is relatively widespread—up to 24 percent of the population, according to Paul Ray, and possibly growing. The evidence suggests, therefore, that conversion to Soka Gakkai is best understood as giving expression to previously held values rather than a dramatic transformation of world-view; those who convert are not randomly drawn from the population at large but come out of a sub-population who, metaphorically at least, "demand" a religion reflecting transmodern values.

Chances are, affiliating with other people who share these values serves to reinforce them, which may have the effect of reinforcing the transmodern character of converts to SGI-USA. In other words, involvement in Soka Gakkai might systematize what before was a loose set of social attitudes, making the pattern more vivid among converts than would have been the case before they joined SGI. The result is a world-view that existed to some degree before, but is now coherent and endowed with sacred meaning. Conversion, therefore, expresses social values already held, reinforces them through association with like-minded others, and legitimates them with a Buddhist religious tradition.

Religious conversion is commonly perceived as a clean break with tradition. That perception is understandable when individuals raised in one religious tradition adopt another that appears very different. That picture may apply to many conversion experiences, but analysis of converts to SGI-USA suggests that they are not so much breaking with American cultural traditions as they are participating in a revitalization movement—a movement not rejecting American culture but reinterpreting it.

Like the Protestant ethic long dominant in America, transmodern culture also expresses an inner-worldly asceticism that endows the mundane world of daily life with religious significance. However, transmodern asceticism is more attuned to the experience of life in a consumer-oriented society. Rather than encouraging individuals to practice self-denial, thrift, and deferred gratification, the transmodern ascetic pursues self-fulfillment as a means to a greater common good. Whereas modernist culture tends to classify and separate things, including people, according to their differences, transmodernism celebrates differences as contributing to the whole. Further, it promotes a sense of relationship between self and other, which extends not only to other human beings but also to the natural and physical world. And whereas the culture of modernism tends to reject things of the past in the hope of new and better things to come, transmodernism looks to the future with optimism but turns to the wisdom of ancient religions for guidance on how to proceed.

Given this cultural reorientation, it is not difficult to understand the appeal of Soka Gakkai to people who are part of this emerging transmodern subculture. By interpreting personal success as a sign of "human revolution" taking place in individuals' lives, Soka Gakkai endows the gratification of personal desires with religious meaning and moral sanction. The idea of karma, however, encourages participants to think about personal benefits in terms of their impact on others, providing a check on the moral license seemingly granted to members. A religion with a distinctively humanist edge, Soka Gakkai affirms the potential of human progress but draws upon the wisdom of Buddhist tradition for insight into the responsible uses of modernity's products.

Because Soka Gakkai Buddhism shares many of these characteristics with other religions that can also be described as transmodern, it faces competition. However, the potential market for transmodern religion is large and possibly growing. If Ray is correct in his estimation that up to 24 percent of the US population now share the transmodern viewpoint, then Soka Gakkai has probably not yet reached its potential for growth in the United States. SGI-USA, along with other religions in the transmodern family, can hope for a promising future.

6

Encounter, Recruitment, and Conversion

IN 1996, 1 out of every 8 respondents to the General Social Survey replied "none" when asked about their religious preference. This means that about 12 percent of all Americans are unchurched and, in a sense, potentially available for recruitment to a religious organization. In the last chapter, we learned that up to 24 percent of all Americans fit the "trans-modern" value profile. Taken together, therefore, about 3 of every 100 people (12 percent × 24 percent) SGI-USA members encounter randomly in their daily lives are potential recruits to Soka Gakkai Buddhism. Of course, there are other, non-random circumstances influencing the likelihood that an encounter with a Soka Gakkai member will result in recruitment. In this chapter, we explore some of these factors.

We begin by demonstrating that at the time of their first encounter with Soka Gakkai, most converts were available for recruitment to a religious organization. This availability often took the form of what David Snow called "structural."[1] That is, when they encountered Soka Gakkai, most of these converts were at a time in their lives when they were relatively free of social ties, such as family obligations and careers. But converts were also *religiously* available at the time of their first encounter with SGI. Although the evidence is somewhat sparse in this

---

[1] Snow, Shakubuku.

regard, most converts appear to have already left the religion in which they were raised, and there is reason to believe that most were not firmly incorporated in any other religion at the time. In short, when they were presented the opportunity to learn about Soka Gakkai Buddhism, they had no pressing reason to decline the invitation.

Next, we demonstrate that converts were often in relatively close proximity to Soka Gakkai. Not only were they structurally available, but most also had some structural connection with SGI-USA members, usually through friends or family members. In fact, as already mentioned in Chapter 4, it was through these social ties that converts first encountered Soka Gakkai. In value orientation as well, many converts appear to have had a certain proximity to Soka Gakkai Buddhism; many of these converts were already moving in the direction of alternative religious forms before encountering Soka Gakkai. In fact, many had explored other religions that share some of Soka Gakkai's "transmodern" characteristics.

Obviously, these generalizations do not apply uniformly to everyone who knows a Soka Gakkai member and accepts an invitation to learn more about the religion. There is variation, in other words, in the *degree* to which converts were available for recruitment and tending toward SGI-USA when that first encounter occurred. Nonetheless, it is safe to say that people who encounter Soka Gakkai and have these characteristics in some combination are more likely to be successfully recruited than people who do not.

Furthermore, not everyone who is successfully recruited—in the sense that they agree to attend Soka Gakkai meetings and learn about the religion—will ultimately convert. In fact, most do not. As is the case with all new religions, attrition among new recruits to SGI-USA is very high. This observation raises another question, therefore: what factors determine whether recruitment will result in conversion? Using the measure of involvement developed in Chapter 3, we attempt here to discover differences between those current members who appear most likely to defect (marginal members) and those who appear to be most confirmed in the religion (core members).

It is useful, then, to speak of encounter, recruitment, and conversion as analytically distinct stages in becoming a Soka Gakkai member. In reality, of course, the markers that determine when individuals have moved from one stage to the next are not entirely clear. As the discussion proceeds, it will become apparent that religious conversion is a process, a process that for many of these converts began long before their first encounter with Soka Gakkai, and continues still. Furthermore, the outcome of this process is not fixed. While many converts to Soka Gakkai find in the religion a permanent spiritual home, others eventually leave SGI-USA and move on to other things. We conclude this chapter with a brief sketch of the defection process.

As in all discussions of the process of religious conversion, this chapter must be read with a degree of caution. Retrospective accounts of how and why people join a new religion often take the form of *post hoc* rationalizations. That is not to say that people act on such an important decision as changing religious affiliation without thinking about it first. In fact, we shall have occasion to discuss the motivating logic behind conversion to Soka Gakkai in this chapter. It is to say, however, that converts often rehearse formulaic accounts of the conversion experience—of the "I once was lost, but now I'm found" variety, for instance. In this study, we attempted to minimize the instance of such accounts by asking about specific kinds of experience at the time of the respondents' first encounter with Soka Gakkai. Nonetheless, it must be kept in mind that the respondents' answers are based on recollections of experiences that occurred in the past.

Availability for Recruitment

Among the most significant findings by researchers looking into the conversion process in the 1970s was the role of social, as opposed to cognitive or emotional, processes associated with religious conversion. The interpersonal aspects of the conversion process were described well by David Snow, in an earlier study of conversion to Soka Gakkai in the United States.[2] He found that converts were "structurally available" for recruitment when they encountered SGI-USA (then Nichiren Shoshu Academy, or NSA). Our data confirm this generalization, but what does this mean?

Converts to SGI, at the time of their first encounter with the religion, were often not yet employed in full-time jobs. Fourteen percent report being unemployed at the time. Another 11 percent were full-time students. Twenty percent were employed only part-time. According to these data, close to half of the converts did not have full-time job commitments that would have restricted the amount of time they could devote to exploring religion.

These converts were often unencumbered in terms of personal relationships as well. Only 32 percent report that they were married or living with a partner at the time of their first encounter with SGI. Furthermore, 43 percent report that they were not living in the same geographic area as their parents or siblings when the encounter occurred.

These findings do not, however, mean that converts were socially isolated or marginalized when they encountered SGI. (Only 20 percent said they felt lonely prior to joining SGI.) Rather, most of them were simply at an age when lack of such obligations is typical. Sixty-one percent were under the age of 30 when they first learned about Soka Gakkai. Given their young age, it is not surprising to find that they were not yet employed in full-time occupations or married, or that they were geographically mobile. The evidence thus qualifies most converts as structurally available for recruitment when they encountered SGI. That is, they were able to move around freely in the social world, relatively free of personal obligations.

[2] Snow, *Shakubuku.*

A similar pattern may be observed in regard to religious availability. It makes sense to think that people who are actively involved in a religion would be unlikely converts to a very different religion. Sociologists have demonstrated that, while switching from one religious denomination to another is common, conversion to a completely different religion is relatively rare. Most of the time, religious mobility occurs within religious "families."[3] That is, people who are raised in one liberal Protestant denomination and switch are likely to switch to another liberal Protestant denomination, as opposed to a conservative denomination, or Catholicism. Indeed, it is because of the relative rarity of radical religious conversion that the growth of alternative religions in mid-twentieth-century America captured the attention of scholars, to say nothing of concerned relatives. It turns out that, for the most part, radical conversion follows a period of religious disaffiliation. That is, people join a new religion only after they have already dropped out of the old one.

In retrospect, we committed an error of oversight by failing to ask whether, at the time of their first encounter with SGI, converts were active in any other religious organization. Nevertheless, it can be inferred from the evidence available that few if any converts were firmly incorporated in a religion when they first encountered Soka Gakkai.

Thirty percent of the converts in the sample report that, before joining SGI, they had been involved in at least one religion other than the religion in which they were raised. This pattern of religious mobility suggests that many of these converts were unattached to any religion prior to joining SGI, or were at least open to religious change. In fact, when asked to describe whether they were religious prior to joining SGI, the converts responded in a manner suggesting a private spirituality not associated with organized religion at all. This response, Roof sug-

---

[3] Wade Clark Roof and William McKinney, *American Mainline Religion: Its Changing Shape and Future* (New Brunswick, NJ: Rutgers University Press, 1987), 166–7.

Table 38. Religious availability prior to conversion (%)

Indicators of religiosity	SGI-USA Converts
Had been involved in a religion other than the one in which respondent was raised	30
Religiosity prior to conversion:	
Very religious	20
Spiritual but not religious	55
Not religious or spiritual	19
Other response:	
Actively seeking	2
Somewhat religious	2
Atheist, agnostic, or opposed to religion	1
Other	3
N	323

Note: Questions 11 and 12 in the questionnaire, App. C.

gests, is characteristic of Baby Boomers and distinguishable from the "religiousness" associated with participation in an organized religion.[4] This "spiritual" response was chosen by 55 percent of the converts (Table 38). Nineteen percent replied that they were not concerned about religion or spirituality at the time. Only 20 percent of the converts described themselves as "very religious" prior to joining SGI. Altogether, these data suggest that most converts were religiously available when they encountered SGI in the sense that, although they might have been interested in religious matters, they were not attached to any particular religious organization.

An interesting pattern emerges when responses to this question are cross-tabulated by whether converts had a history of religious switching. Those converts in the sample who described themselves as "very religious" were more likely than the others to have had prior religious involvement (Table 39).

[4] Roof, *A Generation of Seekers*.

147

Table 39. Switching and prior religiosity

Religiosity	Had been involved in other religions prior to SGI	
	%	N
Very religious	40	77
Spiritual, not religious	28	180
Not spiritual or religious	7	94
Other	42	43

Notes: Questions 11 and 12 in the questionnaire, App. C.
Chi-squared = 30.041, df = 3, p <0.000.

This finding supports Roof's notion that, in the minds of survey respondents, "religiousness" is associated with participation in organized religion, while "spirituality" connotes a religious interest detached from organized religion. It also suggests two different ways that converts were religiously available for recruitment. Either they considered themselves spiritual in a private sense, unattached to organized religion, or they were religious in a manner oriented to organized religion, but not committed to any particular religion at the time of encounter. In one of two ways, therefore, the majority of SGI-USA converts were available for religious recruitment when they first encountered SGI.

Being free to explore religiously—that is, having the time and the freedom to experiment with different religions—clearly increases the chances that an encounter will lead to recruitment. Nonetheless, not having a reason to decline an offer to attend an SGI gathering is not sufficient reason to accept such an invitation. No doubt there are many people who are available in these ways who nevertheless decline such opportunities. Therefore we explore next some other factors that raise the odds of recruitment.

Proximity to Soka Gakkai

If being available for recruitment were all there was to say about people's likelihood of joining a new religion, we would expect the conversion process to be random. But that is not the case; people who are structurally available for recruitment do not simply convert to the first religious group that approaches them. Other factors are involved.

One such factor is the presence of pre-existing social ties. People are more likely to join a group if they already know people who are involved in that group. This factor might be described as structural proximity, as distinct from structural availability.

As noted in Chapter 4, very few converts to SGI joined after being approached by a stranger. Most were first introduced to Soka Gakkai by some pre-existing acquaintance. The most common means of exposure was through a friend (38 percent; Table 40). Since few of the converts reported living in the same area as other members of their family, it is not surprising that converts report being introduced by a member of their immediate family only half as often (19 percent). As noted in Chapter 4, even among those who marked "other" in response to this

Table 40. How converts first encountered SGI-USA (%)

Means of encounter	SGI-USA Converts
Through my spouse (or future spouse)	5
Through a member of my family	14
Through a work colleague	13
Through a friend	38
Through a casual acquaintance	15
At an exhibition or concert	1
By literature or publicity	1
Some other means	14
N	317

Note: Question 4 in the questionnaire, App. C.

question, the role of pre-existing social ties to SGI is evident in about half of those cases. Only 6 out of 317 converts learned about SGI through public exhibitions sponsored by SGI or some other impersonal means.

On closer examination, the structural proximity of converts to SGI at the *time of their encounter* with the religion is striking. Twenty-two percent reported that at least one person in their family was a member of Soka Gakkai before they themselves joined. Furthermore, when describing how they came to be *involved* in SGI, the continuing role of interpersonal ties is evident. Twenty-one percent of the converts said they had gotten acquainted with one or more SGI members who impressed them so much that they decided to get involved (Table 41). Another 18 percent said they got involved reluctantly to please

Table 41. How converts first got involved in SGI (%)

Pattern of recruitment	SGI-USA Converts
I had heard and read enough about SGI to know that I wanted to get involved	4
I got acquainted with one or more SGI members who impressed me so much that I decided to get involved	21
Almost by chance, I was invited to an SGI meeting, was immediately impressed, and got involved	12
I got involved reluctantly to please someone else, but then I saw what chanting could do, so I got involved	18
I was curious, so I tried practicing, liked the results, and got involved	35
Other	10
N	319

Note: Questions 7 in the questionnaire, App. C.

someone else, were impressed with the results of chanting, and decided to get involved. Thirty-nine percent, therefore, cited interpersonal relationships with members of Soka Gakkai as the primary reason for getting involved. Thirty-five percent cited curiosity, which itself could have been stimulated by an acquaintance with an SGI member. Even many of those 12 percent who said they got involved after a chance encounter could have known the person who invited them. Not really "chance," therefore, but social ties are a key to understanding the recruitment process.

The importance of interpersonal relationships is further evidenced by the converts' descriptions of what they originally found most attractive about SGI-USA. Fifty-two percent of the converts said it was the impressive people they met that attracted them to SGI. Often they expanded their description, saying that the people they met seemed very kind or sincere. Comparatively, only 28 percent said they were attracted to SGI because of the promise of benefits. Even fewer mentioned being impressed by SGI's philosophy, goals, or activities (10 percent).

Notably, only 4 percent said they knew enough about Soka Gakkai to join at the time of first encounter. Most knew just enough about the religion to take an interest in learning more. Thus, describing their first reaction to what they observed in their initial encounter with Soka Gakkai, only 21 percent said they were reluctant or skeptical and about the same number said that they reacted with "immediate enthusiasm" (24 percent). Most of the converts said they reacted with "some interest" (40 percent).

Through their existing or developing acquaintances with other Soka Gakkai members, most of the converts apparently learned enough about the religion to stimulate an interest in learning more. Few approached the encounter blindly, with no prior knowledge of what they would experience. Still, the primary reason most of the converts got involved was not the appeal of chanting and the benefits promised. Rather, the attraction is best understood as a positive response to Soka Gakkai members.

But, as we have already said, converts were in relatively close proximity to Soka Gakkai *religiously* as well. It was noted earlier that about 30 percent of the converts had engaged in a pattern of religious switching prior to joining SGI. The religions in which these converts had been involved are telling. While various mainstream denominations were mentioned more frequently than any other religious group (43 percent had switched to one of these denominations), nearly that many (38 percent) had been involved in one of the new religions, such as ISKCON, Zen, Bahai, neo-paganism, or Transcendental Meditation. The next most frequently mentioned religions were marginal Christian bodies, such as Christian Science, Mind Science, and Unity (22 percent). Notably, these latter two categories include many groups that share Soka Gakkai's "transmodern" emphasis on healing and wholeness, the oneness of the spiritual and material worlds, and the attempt to reconcile religion and science. Sixty percent of the converts who had switched to religions other than the one in which they were raised, therefore, show a pattern of movement toward religions with "transmodern" characteristics.

In addition to the evidence of movement toward alternative religions among religious converts, other evidence suggests a prior interest in Eastern religions specifically. About 38 percent of the converts indicated that prior to joining SGI, they had encountered some form of Buddhism or other Eastern religion. Twenty-five percent said they were "very interested in Eastern religion and philosophy." An impressive 47 percent said they had a prior interest in Japan or things Japanese, such as Japanese cuisine, language, or graphic arts. This openness to foreign cultures is further evidenced by the large proportion of converts who had traveled outside of the United States prior to joining SGI (66 percent), and/or read about non-Western cultures (43 percent; Table 42). While comparable data for the American public are not available, it is doubtful that the proportion of

Americans exhibiting these kinds of interest in Eastern culture would be this high.

An interesting pattern emerges when interest in Eastern religion is cross-tabulated with experience in psychotherapy. Most converts answered "no" to both questions, but only 7 percent said they had explored both. This means that the pattern of self-searching exhibited by over a third of the converts took *either* the form of secular psychotherapy *or* an interest in Eastern religion, but not both. Which path these converts took in their self-exploration was related to the way they described their religiosity prior to joining SGI. Those who described themselves as spiritual but not religious were more likely to have expressed a prior interest in Eastern religion, to have actually encountered another religion of Eastern origin, and to have traveled outside of the United States before joining SGI-USA. Those who described themselves as neither spiritual nor religious were the least likely to have explored any of these alternatives, including psychotherapy. Most likely to have explored psychotherapy were those few who marked "other" in response to the question about religiosity. Forty percent of those respondents who described themselves as actively seeking, religiously lukewarm, or opposed to religion (the primary "other"

Table 42. Religious proximity prior to conversion (%)

Indicators of proximity	SGI-USA Converts
Had encountered other forms of Eastern religion:	38
Other forms of Buddhism	27
Other forms of Eastern religion	25
Very interested in Eastern religion and philosophy	25
Interested in Japan or things Japanese	47
Had traveled outside of the United States	66
Had read about non-Western cultures	43
N	320

Notes: Questions 15, 13, and 14 in the questionnaire, App. C.

responses) had undertaken psychotherapy prior to encountering SGI, compared to only 23 percent of those who said they were very religious or spiritual, and 10 percent of those who said they were just not concerned about religion at the time.

These data demonstrate not only that most converts to SGI-USA were not committed to any religious organization prior to encountering Soka Gakkai, but also that most were in relatively close proximity to a religion of Eastern origin. Most had already given up on the mainstream options available to them in the United States, and many appear to have been actively exploring alternatives. The majority exhibits an orientation to inner, personal spirituality and a search for self-awareness that led many to explore Eastern religions or psychotherapy before finding in Soka Gakkai a set of beliefs and practices that satisfied their demands. The data reveal a clear pattern of movement, therefore, away from the mainstream religions in which converts were raised and toward alternatives that often had roots in Eastern religion.

The most likely candidates for recruitment to Soka Gakkai, therefore, are people who (1) are not only available for recruitment in the sense that they are free to join a new group, but (2) are also interested in Eastern religion and (3) are familiar with Soka Gakkai through at least one acquaintance with a member. Of course, as already noted, there is variation in the degree to which individual converts resembled this model candidate at the time of their first encounter with Soka Gakkai. And, as is the case in sociological models generally, there are factors that influence recruitment that we have not considered. Recruitment, like conversion, is a process that takes more time and effort for some people than others. Nonetheless, these findings help us to understand better why recruitment efforts are more successful with some people than with others.

Becoming an Active Member

Not everyone who is recruited to Soka Gakkai becomes active in the religion. Most do not. Using the measure of involvement developed in Chapter 3, we now attempt to discover why some people become very involved in SGI while others remain marginal to the life of the organization and appear at risk of defection. Obviously, all of these respondents represent converts, in the sense that they joined SGI and are currently active members. It would be impossible, in a random sample drawn from subscriptions to SGI publications, to tap a sufficient number of people who joined for a while, decided Soka Gakkai was not right for them, and dropped out. We did attempt to make contact with ex-members in the process of conducting follow-up interviews but were able to reach only five. It makes sense, however, to regard those respondents classified as marginal—some of whom appear to be at risk of defection—as having something in common with those who dropped out. These respondents, therefore, can be used as surrogates for drop-outs, making it possible to examine the reasons that some recruits become confirmed converts, while others do not.

Demographic Associations

Demographic variables do very little to explain degrees of involvement. Only two such variables—age and whether one has ever been divorced—reduced the level of uncertainty in predicting degree of involvement. Gender, employment status, income, race, current marital status, education, and region are not associated with differences in involvement.

As might be expected, members in the oldest birth cohort (born before 1946) were most likely to be core SGI-USA members (19 percent), followed by the middle birth cohort (born 1946–62; 14 percent). Only one respondent in the youngest birth cohort (born since 1962) was classified as a core SGI-USA member. It should not be concluded, however, that youth itself causes SGI recruits to lose interest and drop out. Rather, differences in degree of involvement reflect the length of time respondents have been involved in SGI-USA. On average, respondents in the youngest cohort have been involved in

SGI-USA for about 12 years, compared to 18 years for the middle cohort and 24 years for the oldest cohort. Understandably, the longer persons have been involved in SGI, the greater the likelihood they will stay. This pattern can be interpreted as a consequence of the tendency of less enthusiastic members to drop out, leaving, over time, those members who are most committed (as described in Chapter 3).

The relationship between divorce and involvement is not so easily explained. Converts to SGI-USA who have been divorced are less likely than those who have not been divorced to be core members, but they are also less likely to be marginal. Most of them fall into the middle, "general" member category. Such a contradictory pattern suggests the influence of some underlying variable related *both* to divorce *and* to involvement; and the obvious candidate is whether these converts became involved in Soka Gakkai through marriage to an SGI-USA member. Indeed, there is some evidence to support this hypothesis. Converts who are not married to an SGI member are more likely to be marginal (29 percent vs. 11 percent of those married to a member). Those respondents whose spouse is a member and who joined after their spouse did, suggesting that they married into the religion, are less likely to be core members than those who joined before their spouse (12 percent vs. 38 percent). Of the members who said they were first introduced by their spouses but are currently divorced none is a core member. This suggests that, while marriage to another SGI member can work to enhance involvement (as evidenced by the lower probability of finding marginal members among married SGI couples), those who joined SGI in order to please their spouses have less reason to continue in the religion if those marriages end.

Apart from these special cases—age and divorce—demographic characteristics are of little help in understanding involvement.

Experiences in SGI

If demographic characteristics that recruits bring with them into Soka Gakkai do not explain the depth of their involvement, then perhaps certain experiences since their initial SGI encounter do. The results of an analysis along this line are somewhat more promising.

Interpersonal relationships, which we know to be a determining factor in recruitment, also play a role in determining long-term involvement. Those respondents who were originally attracted to Soka Gakkai by the people they met were less likely to be marginal members than those who were not so attracted (19 percent vs. 34 percent). Responses to a related question support this interpretation. Respondents were asked how important the support of other members has been to their own practice. Those who said that they did not rely on the support of others were more likely to be marginal members (44 percent), while those who said the support of other members was very important to them were the least likely to fall into the marginal category (21 percent).

It makes sense to think that recruits to Soka Gakkai are more likely to become actively involved if they enjoy the company of other members. However, because the number of friends and family members who are Soka Gakkai members is a part of the involvement measure, the positive correlation between these two variables is difficult to interpret. Causation could go either way and probably goes both ways.

Other kinds of experience are more telling. It might be thought, for instance, that recruits who experience strong negative reactions by family and friends to their involvement would be more likely to limit their involvement. For the most part, however, that is not the case. As already noted, most of the respondents who had experienced negative reactions from others also minimized the experience. Only the experience of negative reactions by the respondent's spouse was significantly associated with involvement; such persons tended to gravitate toward the marginal category. Negative reactions by parents, siblings, and friends had no demonstrable effect on involvement.

The survey was conducted just six years after the schism with Nichiren Shoshu, and members are still adjusting to Soka Gakkai's new independence. While the priesthood never played a major role for most American members, the schism nonetheless had an impact on involvement. Those 52 respondents who said that they thought SGI had suffered from the schism were more than three times more likely to be marginal than the 154 who said SGI is better off (43 percent vs. 13 percent). They were also more likely to be marginally involved than those who said the schism made no difference (28 percent). While only 13 out of 320 respondents indicated that they had maintained some connection with the temple, usually through friendships with former Soka Gakkai members who remained loyal to the priests, none of these respondents was a core member. Seven of these 13 respondents were classified as marginal to SGI-USA.

Belief in the possibility of world peace has one of the strongest associations with involvement (Table 43). Half of those respondents who said world peace is not a realistic goal were marginally involved in SGI, compared to 15 percent of those who said world peace is a realistic goal. In fact, none of the 7 respondents who said world peace is not at all realistic was classified as a core member. Comparatively, those who said

Table 43. Involvement and the goal of world peace

Reply	Marginal	
	%	N
Very realistic	15	185
Pretty realistic	37	93
Not very realistic	50	24
Not at all realistic	43	7

Notes: Question 41 in the questionnaire, App. C.

world peace is a very realistic goal were the most likely to be core members. Seventy-seven percent of core members hold that belief, while only 36 percent of marginal members do. Note that not only is it likely that holding strongly to such a belief would lead to greater involvement, but also core involvement no doubt reinforces that belief.

Given the fact that virtually all of the respondents reported experiencing benefits as a result of chanting, this variable had no impact on involvement. That does not mean that the efficacy of chanting plays no role in determining the outcome of recruits' encounters with Soka Gakkai, because chanting for goals that *were not realized* did have an impact on involvement. Those respondents who had this negative experience were twice as likely to be only marginally involved in Soka Gakkai (26 percent) as those who said that they had realized all of their goals (13 percent). Furthermore, among those persons who reported some failure in chanting, those who accepted the idea that their goals had not been realized because they are still undergoing human revolution—the correct doctrinal explanation, so to speak—were least likely to be marginal members (20 percent). Seven out of the 9 (78 percent) who said their goals were not realized because chanting sometimes does not work—the heretical explanation—are marginal members, as are 37 out of 129 (29 percent) who gave other reasons.

Overall, then, interpersonal relationships play less of a role in determining long-term involvement than they play in recruitment. The converts' values, particularly in regard to world peace and acceptance of Soka Gakkai beliefs about chanting, appear to be the primary correlates of involvement. It may be that for those converts who think of their involvement with SGI-USA as yielding inconspicuous benefits, the experience of conspicuous benefits is less necessary for sustained commitment. For some of the converts, however, getting the desired results from chanting is a determining factor, and failure tends to move them to the margins of Soka Gakkai. This appears to be the case, however, for only a small proportion of the converts.

The Costs and Rewards of Conversion

Conversion to a new religion often leads to tension with family members, friends, and sometimes work colleagues, who may be disturbed by what can seem like a sudden change in an individual's language and behavior. People who decide to join a new religion, therefore, must accept certain risks. Furthermore, since the convert must learn the beliefs, language, and practices of the new religion, the conversion process requires a certain investment of time and effort. These risks of tension and potential ostracism, plus the investment of time and effort, may be thought of as the "costs" of religious conversion.

At the same time, conversion offers potential rewards. For instance, in the case of religious intermarriage, tension over which religious tradition to observe in the home, or which to teach the children, can be reduced if one of the partners agrees to convert to the religion of the other. Because religious observance requires time and money (tithing, for instance), observing one tradition in a household, as opposed to two, constitutes a more efficient use of limited resources. We have already discussed other kinds of reward that may be unique to religious practice—for example, the hope for future rewards, such as eternal life, enlightenment, or good karma.

Recently, a team of scholars have turned to a theory of human decision-making basic to economic analysis and applied it to religious decision-making. Rational choice theory, as it is called, is based on the fundamental maxim that *"humans seek what they perceive to be rewards and try to avoid what they perceive to be costs."*[5] The challenge to social analysts who would assess the adequacy of this theory is to weigh the costs and rewards associated with any decision to see if the choice made is in fact rational.

Applying rational choice theory to religious behavior is therefore fraught with difficulties. Perhaps the most significant diffi-

---

[5] Stark and Bainbridge, *The Future of Religion*, 5; emphasis in the original. See also Laurence Iannaccone, "Religious Practice: A Human Capital Approach," *Journal for the Scientific Study of Religion*, 29/3 (1990), 297–314.

culty such an analysis presents is the absence of a standard unit of measurement—equivalent to the dollar—into which the costs and rewards of religious behavior can be translated. For instance, how much of a perceived improvement in one's karma is sufficient to compensate for tensions that may arise in one's family in response to conversion? This difficulty is alleviated somewhat by the qualification contained in the maxim cited above; focusing on the *perception* of costs and rewards makes the analysis possible. But this strategy requires two assumptions that may or may not be warranted: (1) respondents perceive costs and rewards *accurately*, and (2) they report those perceptions *honestly*. Despite these limitations, rational choice theory provides some insight into the SGI-USA conversion process.

It was noted earlier that when converts joined SGI, they were, in many ways, free to move around in the social world. This structural freedom served to minimize the cost of conversion in terms of the risk of tension in family relationships. Because most converts were single at the time, the costs associated with religious intermarriage were largely absent. Furthermore, since many of the converts were living at some geographic distance from parents and siblings, the risk of tension in these relationships could be deferred until the converts were sure about their decision to join. If they thought parents or siblings would react negatively to their joining SGI, they could simply not reveal their new religious identity right away. And since many of the converts were not yet employed in full-time occupations, the potential for problems at work was also minimized.

Even so, 60 percent of the converts said they had experienced difficulties or negative reactions from relatives and friends because of their decision to join SGI-USA. Most often these negative reactions came from the converts' parents (37 percent), or other members of their family, such as in-laws (25 percent). More rarely, converts experienced negative reactions from siblings (14 percent), spouses (12 percent), or friends (20 percent). Difficulties with children and coworkers were mentioned very infrequently (2 percent and 4 percent, respectively), though of course the high rate of converts who were unmarried when they joined SGI-USA and the low rate who were employed full-time act to keep these percentages low. As mentioned already, however, most of the respondents minimized the significance of these reactions. They told us that these people reacted negatively or with suspicion at first—worried, for instance, that the respondent had joined a "cult"—but changed their attitude once they saw the positive impact the respondents' involvement in SGI was having.[6]

Probably the most significant cost associated with conversion to SGI is the amount of time and effort required learning how to chant. SGI-USA offers an instructional video and cassette tape to assist new members, but, even so, learning the chant is a sizeable task.

What motivates such an investment? The answer is not as clear as one would expect, given Soka Gakkai's emphasis on the benefits of chanting. As noted in the sections on structural availability and proximity, the primary *attraction* cited by 52 percent of the converts was not the promise of benefits but positive feelings toward the people they met. When asked what is *now* the most appealing quality of Soka Gakkai, attraction to members drops to 34 percent. The major attraction now is the benefits of chanting plus the "goals and philosophy" of SGI (48 percent). Clearly, the experience of benefits, plus the adoption of SGI ideology, increase with time in the movement and surpass friendship as the major reason to remain in SGI. In other words, the attractiveness of personal relationships, so important at the time of initial contact, fades in *relative* importance as converts become better acquainted with SGI doctrine and practice.

Relative to the apparent costs of involvement in Soka Gakkai, the apparent rewards come to seem great. Perhaps initially most converts invest the time and energy required to learn the prac-

---

[6] Or, it may be more accurate to say, the impact conversion *wasn't* having—that is, the fact that radical changes in behavior did not accompany conversion to SGI.

tice in order to enjoy the company of the people in SGI-USA, but over time those who stay find other, more official rewards more important. Whether this makes conversion to SGI a "rational" choice may be impossible to know, but it can be surmised that at least most converts perceive that the rewards outweigh the costs.

A Note about Orientations to Social Action

Readers familiar with sociological theory will notice that the above analysis of conversion to Soka Gakkai involves three of the four major orientations to social action described by Max Weber.[7] One of the four Weber called traditional action, which "lies very close to the borderline of what can justifiably be called meaningfully oriented action," in that "it is very often a matter of almost automatic reaction to habitual stimuli which guide behaviour in a course which has been repeatedly followed."[8] Obviously, converts to an alternative religion do not participate out of mere habit; conversion involves learning *new* behaviors. Therefore the analysis here does not involve traditional action, but it does touch on the other three.

One type of social action, called *affektuell* by Weber, is based on an affective, or emotional, orientation—to an individual or to a group of people. We have already demonstrated the significance of interpersonal ties and emotional responses to other people in the process of conversion to Soka Gakkai. Converts clearly had a positive emotional response to the people they met through Soka Gakkai. In fact, the role of positive feelings toward other members appears so strong that one could justifiably conclude that the development of positive feelings toward members of the group is almost a necessary precondition to conversion.

Conversely, positive feelings toward people outside of the group one is considering joining may act to inhibit conversion.

---

[7] Max Weber, *The Theory of Social and Economic Organization*, trans. Talcott Parsons (New York: Free Press, 1947).

[8] Ibid. 116.

Knowing that loved ones might respond negatively to a change in religious loyalty might prevent potential recruits from getting involved in a new religion, even if they found it personally appealing. As we have seen, however, Soka Gakkai converts were relatively free of such countervailing interpersonal ties.

Weber called the next orientation to social action *Wertrationalität*, or action based on a logic of absolute values, such as "the action of persons who, regardless of possible cost to themselves, act to put into practice their convictions of what seems to them to be required by duty, honour, the pursuit of beauty, a religious call, personal loyalty, or the importance of some 'cause' no matter in what it consists."[9] Our analysis of religious availability and proximity, combined with the transmodern value orientation found among many converts, suggests that conversion to Soka Gakkai must also be understood as a function of the individual's personal religious desires, beliefs, and values. Most converts had already given up on the more usual American religions and were leaning toward Eastern religious alternatives when they first encountered Soka Gakkai. They apparently found in Soka Gakkai a set of religious beliefs, practices, and values consistent with their own. While pre-existing values appear to play a role secondary to feelings of attraction to other SGI-USA members in the *recruitment* stage, such values play a stronger role in determining whether recruits eventually *convert* to Soka Gakkai Buddhism, and stronger yet in who becomes a core member. In particular, recruits who accept the goal of world peace as realistic are more likely to become confirmed converts to Soka Gakkai than those whose involvement is based on the desire for conspicuous benefits.

The third type of social action is the rough equivalent of the maxim at the base of rational choice theory: humans seek what they perceive to be rewards and avoid what they perceive to be costs. Weber called it *zweckrational* and described it as action "oriented to a system of discrete individual ends when the end,

---

[9] Ibid.

the means, and the secondary results are all rationally taken in account and weighed."[10] In fact, much of Weber's research was concerned with describing how this kind of utilitarian logic was coming to dominate social action in modern societies, a process he referred to as "rationalization," as exemplified in modern bureaucracy. Much of the controversy over the applicability of economic theories—specifically, rational choice theory—to religious behavior involves this third type of social action. As noted above, analyzing religious behavior in terms of rational choices suffers from the lack of a common metric into which the costs and rewards can be translated. Qualifying the maxim to say that it is the "perception" of costs and rewards that influences human decision-making makes a rational choice analysis possible, but, as we pointed out, a more serious consideration is whether a rational choice analysis of religious behavior accurately portrays the motivating logic. Did the religious actors really consider the potential costs and rewards in making their decision, or, more specifically, did the actors choose that behavior as a means to achieve some particular result? And did the religious persons accurately represent their reasoning to the researcher? In other words, is religious conversion a rational choice?

Often, the answer is probably "no." When describing their motivations, most religious people will cite reasons of deeply held convictions or loyalties to their family or ethnic heritage. For the most part, therefore, religious behavior, as Weber himself noted, is expressive of *wertrational* (absolute value) and *affektuell* (emotional) motivations. In the case of conversion to Soka Gakkai, however, the rhetoric of the religion itself demands that we consider the possibility that conversion is motivated by utilitarian concerns. In fact, Soka Gakkai publications advertise its beliefs as verifiable and scientific. Members commonly speak of the benefits as "proof" that chanting works, and use the promise of benefits to persuade people to try

---

[10] Ibid. 117.

chanting themselves. The religion itself is rationally organized, and, as discussed in Chapter 1, operates more like a bureaucracy than a traditional religious organization. In these several ways, therefore, Soka Gakkai places a premium on rationality, qualifying it as a very modern religion.

Our analysis reveals, however, that the hope of experiencing benefits as a result of chanting is a secondary motivation in recruitment. And, as we saw above, benefits from chanting replace friendship as the major attraction only later in the process. This suggests, therefore, that converts adopt the group's rhetoric of rationality only as they become more involved in the practice. That is, members may cite the benefits as a *post hoc* reason for their decision to convert and as a means to convince others to join. The actual decision to join, however, appears to be motivated first by feelings of attraction to other members of the group, and second as an expression of personal conviction.

Defection from SGI-USA

We have already mentioned that the majority of people who are recruited to Soka Gakkai never convert. By and large, the high rate of attrition from SGI-USA is a result of people simply dropping out when they discover, after a brief exposure to the religion, that it doesn't "click" with their own religious beliefs and values.[11] The largest portion of people who get acquainted

[11] While the scholarly literature on religious defection does not match that on religious conversion, some exists nevertheless. See M.B. Brinkerhoff and Katheryn L. Burke, "Disaffiliation: Some Notes on 'Falling from the Faith,' " *Sociological Analysis*, 41 (1980), 41–54; David Caplovitz and Fred Sherrow, *The Religious Dropouts* (Beverly Hills, Calif.: Sage, 1977); Janet Jacobs, *Divine Disenchantment* (Bloomington: Indiana University Press, 1989); Armand L. Mauss, "Dimensions of Defection," *Review of Religious Research*, 10 (1969), 128–35; James T. Richardson, *Conversion Careers: In and Out of the New Religions* (Beverly Hillls, Calif.: Sage, 1977); Norman Skonovd, "Apostasy: The Process of Defection from Religious Totalism," Ph.D. thesis (Ann Arbor, Mich.: University Microfilms International, 1981); Stuart A. Wright, *Leaving Cults: The Dynamics of Defection* (Washington: Society for the Scientific Study of Religion, 1987).

with SGI-USA fall into this group of drop-outs. A smaller group, we have argued, find that Soka Gakkai Buddhism speaks to their values and religious demands, and thus they decide to join SGI-USA. Such people may properly be considered converts. But there remains yet a third group, of unknown size, but no less important to our narrative—that is, people who convert to Soka Gakkai Buddhism, but eventually defect from the religion.

Reliable information about defection from a new religion is notoriously difficult to acquire for a number of reasons. First, the number of defectors is usually small compared to either drop-outs or converts. Second, such people rarely maintain contact with the religious group after defecting, making it virtually impossible to locate them through normal channels, such as membership rolls or subscription lists. The most accessible defectors, thirdly, are those that organize into support or advocacy groups of the sort associated with the anti-cult movement. While readily accessible, the information such people provide is suspect.

We were able to interview five people who told us they had dropped out of SGI-USA. One, whom we encountered earlier in this chapter, left quite recently. That is, she decided that Soka Gakkai was not for her, so she gradually stopped attending meetings. Another, who chants regularly, technically never "joined" the Soka Gakkai. She indicated to us that she has studied this and other forms of Buddhism and decided that "it's not necessary to be a member." That leaves only three who may properly be considered defectors. Although this is scant evidence about an important topic, their explanations of why they decided to leave Soka Gakkai, combined with statements made by current members who are wavering in their commitment, allow us to say something about the process of defection from SGI-USA.

We asked the three defectors why they left SGI-USA, whether they were still chanting at the time of the interview, and, if so, why. Finally, we asked these former members to describe their overall feelings toward SGI-USA. Their responses are as follows:

Can you tell us why you left?
It seemed like it was highly structured, regimented to a certain extent. I know they are trying to change for the times, but as an SGI member, you come to start seeing the world through one lens, and I want to be able to see the world through many lenses. They don't really encourage people to study other forms of Buddhism.

I stopped going to their meetings and chanting in January of last year, 1997. . . . I became disillusioned with, not with the practice itself, but the people who were practicing. They were a little too militant for my liking. . . . A number of people started telling me that if I wasn't chanting twice a day, and I wasn't following the regime as they saw fit, then I wasn't doing it correctly. And to me, that went against what we were doing it for. Intolerance didn't seem to be an aspect that I thought was acceptable. And I had also done some readings on Nichiren. It seemed that he was quite militant, too, about trying to force people to practice and excluding all other religions, even other sects of Buddhism, as not being able to reach enlightenment. I don't agree with that. I stopped going to the Soka Gakkai meetings last January. I have since gone to the temple, which is run by the priests. I've been there once, and I've signed up to do the first steps toward receiving Gohonzon from them. But that was probably May of last year, and I haven't followed through with that either.

It wasn't a very long period of time that I stayed with the organization. I can't really remember, to tell you the truth. It's the same with my practice. I drop it and start it. So it goes through periods of not happening.

At this time, are you still chanting? If yes, why?
No.

No. I still have an altar set up, but I don't chant regularly. I do it once in a while if I . . . I have friends who live about fifty miles from here who are members of the temple, and if I go to their place, I will chant with them.

Yes. I don't know [why]. I really don't. I do have a connection with it, and I always come back. And I always enjoy it when I do it. But then I start questioning its worth.

How would you characterize your overall feelings towards SGI?
Positive.

I would say generally negative.

I thought it was very positive. . . . when I went to the meetings and I talked to people, it was a very pleasant experience.

As in conversion, the social aspects of defection are clear in the foregoing statements. In fact, the defection process for these former members appears to be the reverse of the conversion process. Attracted to the people in SGI-USA in the first place, they found in SGI a religion that spoke to their religious demands and agreed to join. Later, when tension with some of the other members arose, they became disaffected, not necessarily with the religion, but with the people. Two of these defectors cite tension with other SGI-USA members—over studying other forms of Buddhism in one case and, on a similar note, over perception of militancy among some members in the other.

These kinds of concern were echoed in statements made by current members who are wavering in their commitment. We have heard already the experience of one member who was offended when his Catholic girlfriend was exposed to anti-Catholic sentiments at an SGI-USA meeting. But consider the following statements as well:

There's just a lot of people that pretty much don't practice what they preach. . . .. These people had sort of established a pecking order, so to speak—"I'm on a faster track to enlightenment than you are because I put more time in. I chant ten hours a night." . . . It seems like the holier-than-thou type people—the "Bible thumpers"—it's just those kinds of people that I care not to listen to. If it works for them, great. But please don't say that I'm having difficulty in my life because I'm not sitting properly when I chant.

The thing that turns me off about the organization is something that turns me off in general. . . . That is when people stray from the true meaning or true purpose of what they're doing. . . . We all go through different things at different times, and sometimes I feel like I can best support these fanatic, crazily-hyped energy people by letting them go through their thing, and just observe them and watch them grow from a distance. . . . I think a lot of times, there's too much emphasis put on . . . "you must chant morning and night." There really are no musts. That's what Buddhism is about. Buddhism is not about rules and regulations.

I remember a kid one time who just started the practice and it was cute. If you want to look down on things, but this wasn't . . . it was just where he was at. He was so excited—poor kid, and he never had too much. He put a dime in one of those [snack] machines and instead of one cupcake, he got two. He was thrilled, sparkling. He was smiling at everything else, and . . . some sophisticated ass would go in and say, "Oh God, how stupid." But see, it wasn't stupid. It was a thrill to that kid. And whatever is a thrill to an individual, whatever does something to uplift them, is worth whatever. And it's not to be smirked at, in my opinion.

Zeal for Soka Gakkai Buddhism can be infectious, raising the overall level of commitment in the organization when others get caught up in the excitement. When that zeal, however, is combined with judgmentalism, competitiveness, and intolerance for other religions, it can have the opposite effect, causing some people to feel uncomfortable, and ultimately leading them to question their commitment to being involved in the collective life of SGI-USA. Many converts came to Soka Gakkai through their spiritual seeking, which often led them through several other religions. Indeed, we have seen that such spiritual seekers are very often the kind of person most likely to find Soka Gakkai Buddhism attractive. To these people, it must be disconcerting to encounter SGI members who express little tolerance for the truths of other religions. And for people who are attracted to Soka Gakkai as a group that supports one another's spiritual growth, the experience of competitiveness and judgmentalism by some members must be confusing.

Out of all the wavering members and people who had defected from SGI-USA to whom we spoke, only one expressed the kinds of criticism that are commonly found in the anti-cult movement. This person, who still chants but is cutting back on his involvement with SGI-USA, had this to say: "I don't feel that SGI is forthcoming about their finances. I have asked questions of leaders and been referred to other people, and rudely did not get a response from anyone. . . . I said it feels like a fiefdom, where we just hand up the money. . . . I don't like to be the rude kid who always asks the uncomfortable questions."

Financial mismanagement has been one of the more common accusations levied against Soka Gakkai by former members now involved in organizations such as Ex-NSA, which is associated with the anti-cult movement. It is notable, however, that such accusations appear only rarely among defectors who are not associated with the anti-cult movement, or among current members, many of whom were forthcoming about other kinds of problems they had experienced in SGI-USA during their interviews. It is also notable that only one former member expressed negative feelings about SGI-USA, and her opinion has no doubt been influenced by affiliation with members of the temple.

For the most part, defection from SGI-USA appears primarily to be a social process, much like the process of recruitment and conversion. Defection is most likely to occur when a member experiences conflict with other members in their local group. Such conflicts, furthermore, appear to be a function of dissonance experienced when people who join SGI-USA in order to pursue spiritual growth in a supportive and relatively free-thinking group encounter competitiveness and judgmentalism. Only one of these people expressed serious doubts about the usefulness of the practice or Soka Gakkai beliefs. Most indicated an intention to continue chanting on their own, although they were thinking about leaving the organization.

In Conclusion

Conversion to Soka Gakkai is far from random. Although we have certainly not exhausted all of the possibilities, the data tells a compelling story about several factors that influence the process of encounter, recruitment, and conversion. More significantly for the thesis we have been developing in this part of the book, recruitment is most likely to result in conversion when the religion being supplied meets the religious demands of potential converts. This fact reveals the importance of interpersonal relationships and values in the process of conversion to SGI-USA. Put in other terms, the costs and rewards of converting to SGI are not fixed but depend upon the recruits' social proximity to SGI-USA and values held by recruits at the time of the encounter. Over time, converts adopt the language of Soka Gakkai Buddhism to express their concerns about the state of life in this world. Furthermore, through the practice of chanting and involvement in Soka Gakkai's efforts to promote peace through culture and education, converts are able to put those convictions into action. Ironically, the members of Soka Gakkai, who play a crucial role in recruitment, are also the deciding factor in the defection process. Having been attracted by the friendly people in the first place, members can become disaffected from the organization by interpersonal conflicts with other members. When this happens, they begin to doubt, not the religion itself, but the value of their involvement with the religious organization.

While converts to Soka Gakkai in the United States appear to be choosing a distinct alternative to the predominately Protestant American culture, they have joined a religion that promotes its own kind of inner-worldliness. Unlike the Calvinist asceticism described by Weber, however, Soka Gakkai promotes a kind of inner-worldliness that gives religious meaning and moral sanction to self-gratification and consumption, couching this consumerism in a concern for the well-being of others. It is an ideology therefore consistent with the experiences of life in contemporary American society. And conversion to Soka Gakkai, if not a "rational choice," is at least an understandable one.

Conclusion

SOKA Gakkai successfully made the transition from being a religion of immigrants to being a competitor in the American religious market. While several other new religions of Eastern origin experienced sudden popularity in the decades of the 1960s and 1970s, then declined as rapidly as they had grown, Soka Gakkai achieved stability, growing quietly into a religious alternative with a promising future in the United States. Explaining the overall success of this new religion—how it gained converts and how it accommodated to life in America—has been the guiding concern of this study. To understand the social conditions and processes that influenced the performance of Soka Gakkai in America, we have drawn on two perspectives that are sometimes at odds in academic debates.

On the supply side, it was demonstrated that certain conditions changed in the mid-1960s, making the American social environment more receptive to religions of Eastern origin. Earlier immigrants who often did not share the Protestant "American" perspective stimulated a period of cultural "contraction," which led to the enactment of laws restricting immigration from Asian countries. These laws were rescinded in the mid-1960s. There followed not only a rise in the number of immigrants from Asian countries, but also an increase in the number of Asian religions in America.

America's religious landscape was changing in other ways as well, and this brings up the demand side of the story. Images of the destructive capacities of technology after two world wars and highly publicized environmental disasters cast a shadow over Americans' optimism and faith in human progress through science. Fascist movements in Europe, and racism and anti-communism in America, had raised awareness of the dangers of populism to a democratic government. The Great Depression and other problems, such as inflation and economic stagnation, challenged Americans' faith in free-market capitalism.

At the same time, Americans were becoming increasingly mobile, not just geographically, but also socially. Rising levels of education and the emergence of a new class of jobs requiring specialized knowledge signaled a shift in the American social structure. One's identity and sense of belonging were no longer automatic, inherited from one's family, or ascribed on the basis of gender or geographic location. Instead, America saw the rise of a meritocracy—a system in which one's position in the social order depends not on *who one is*, but on *what one does* and the choices one makes. Along with these changes came greater individual autonomy in religion and lifestyle, but also, for many, a sense that the meaning systems passed down from earlier generations, significantly informed by Protestant religion and science, were less than certain.

Out of the crisis of meaning attending these challenges emerged a religious awakening but a religious awakening, unlike others in American history. In the past, an awakening had led to a new cultural consensus, but the awakening of the second half of the twentieth century was more an awakening to religious pluralism. However reluctantly, this new awakening forced Americans to rethink what it means to be religious. While some traditionalists held fast to Protestantism as the "true" religion, others, perhaps the majority, came to see that religion could take many forms, each entitled to exist in America.

By the 1960s, this latter perspective was becoming institutionalized in American social habits and federal laws. Religion came to be understood less as a community defined by shared history, doctrine, code, and rituals, and more as an individual way of being in the world. Conviction increasingly took precedence over doctrine. Morality came to be defined, not by conformity with objective rules, but by the honest expression of the self. Techniques for the realization and expression of the self displaced ritual re-enactments of events long past.

The awakening to pluralism was expressed, on a *macrosocial* scale, in what has been described as a further deregulation of religion by the state. Such deregulation is seen both in less restrictive immigration laws and also in Supreme Court decisions identifying individual conscience as what is protected by the First Amendment. *Microsocially*, the awakening to pluralism was expressed in the emergence and spread of what has been called here "transmodernism," a desire for religion oriented to healing—the self certainly (understood as body, mind, and spirit), but also human relationships, relationships with the environment, and relationships with the divine.

Transmodernism itself must be understood less as a break with tradition than as a revitalization of certain American cultural traditions inherited from Protestant religion. Transmodernism shares with that tradition the emphasis on the individual's salvation and personal relationship with the sacred, but it relocates the sacred in the here and now. Thus, the individual's relationship with the sacred is no longer expressed in devotion to a transcendent God but through relationships with nature and one another. This oneness of secular and sacred, material and spiritual, lends itself to a new form of inner-worldly asceticism. As in Protestant religion, the ascetic impulse in transmodern culture is played out in the mundane world, but transmodernism relocates the rewards of hard work and ethical behavior; they are found now not in heaven, but on earth—in the form of prosperity, fulfillment, and happiness.

Transmodernism revitalizes elements of traditional Protestant culture, therefore, in ways consistent with the requirements of an advanced industrial society. Once developed, an industrial society requires a strong market with reliable consumers. Economic stability in an advanced industrial society requires that people consume the goods produced. Too much saving and too little spending results in an oversupply of capital—money, means of production, and unsold goods—and thus economic instability. An advanced industrial society requires a culture that encourages consumption.

It is not difficult to perceive the affinity between the trans-modern ethic, with its emphasis on self-fulfillment in the present world, and the spirit of consumerism, with its emphasis on immediate personal gratification. Transmodernism thus maintains aspects of traditional culture, but it redefines them in light of new social experiences; in America it represents not a break with tradition but a revitalization of the American culture—a process that can be expected to continue.

It is in this context of social and cultural change that the story of Soka Gakkai in the United States can be understood. Religious deregulation made it possible for Soka Gakkai to organize and compete in the American religious market place, but its growth here must also be seen as a response to the trans-modern elements of American culture today.

Those who converted to Soka Gakkai in the USA have been drawn from a segment of the population greatly influenced by the social and cultural changes taking place in twentieth-century America. Young and socially mobile, they have typically experienced a time in their lives when they had the freedom to explore the new variety of religious alternatives available in the United States. Well-educated participants in the new class of information and service occupations, they accepted an ethic of success and actively sought upward mobility. Soka Gakkai's emphasis on taking responsibility for one's own life and taking action to achieve personal goals no doubt spoke to the experience of young professionals in the new meritocracy. At the same time, they were socially progressive—world travelers, interested in and exposed to foreign cultures, their inward, self-orientation balanced by a global consciousness. Religiously, as well, they turned inward, focusing on the inner spiritual realm.

In these many ways, converts to Soka Gakkai in America have been pioneers in an era of dramatic cultural change.

Though solid evidence is sparse as to whether converts had this "transmodern" cultural orientation prior to joining Soka Gakkai, it makes sense to think that Soka Gakkai would appeal disproportionately to those who did. No doubt, for many, this transmodern orientation was, prior to joining, a set of loosely held beliefs and attitudes that became crystallized into a coherent world-view as a result of joining SGI—through joining with others who shared these attitudes in a religion that provided a systematic sacred paradigm. There is little reason to believe that, for these converts, religious conversion entailed a dramatic transformation of world-view. Most continued to see the world in much the same way as they had before, only—through the lens of Soka Gakkai Buddhism—perhaps more clearly.

An equally dramatic conversion story is that of the transformation of Soka Gakkai itself, from a Japanese religion into an American one. Since it was organized in 1960, SGI-USA has undergone a number of changes in organizational structure and practice to improve its position in the American social environment. Often, such changes are seen as resulting from natural, unconscious processes of assimilation or selection. That is, organizations begin to look more American over time as their leaders adopt the habits of American social life and bring those habits into the organization. In this way of thinking, isomorphism (i.e., increasing similarity) stems from the organizational equivalent of the "melting pot." A similar perspective understands the tendency of organizations increasingly to resemble one another as a result of natural selection. That is, given the limitations of the social environment, those organizations that survive will be those best suited to the surrounding conditions; organizations come to resemble one another because those that maintain inefficient practices die off.

In the case of Soka Gakkai, however, organizational change was neither a result of the unconscious assimilation of American habits, nor of random variation and natural selection. It resulted, instead, from conscious policy-making on the part of Soka Gakkai leaders. In this case, neither the melting pot nor a process of evolution accurately reflects the source of organizational change. The more suitable metaphor is that of a competitive market, wherein organizations as players adopt strategic positions relative to other players on the field. Unlike other new religions that adopted a stance of direct opposition to the dominant players and challenged the legitimacy of the widely accepted rules, Soka Gakkai played by the rules and took a more amiable stance. Rather than reject sacred American values such as individualism, capitalism, and the family, Soka Gakkai embraced them. Its leaders consciously instituted a variety of changes to make the organization appear more American. SGI-USA prized legitimacy over efficiency, and over continuity with the mother organization in Japan.

The soft-sell, low-tension strategy may have cost SGI-USA in terms of absolute growth, but that cost, in light of the data on recruitment and conversion, was probably minimal while the payoff was considerable. By adopting this strategy, Soka Gakkai remained distinctive in its beliefs but was not so distinctive as to be perceived as a threat. As such, the religion largely passed unnoticed during the cult scare, making it easier for those who encountered the religion to explore it with little potential cost to themselves. Those who ultimately joined had to give up very little of their former way of life. Conversion, apart from learning to chant, entailed only minor behavioral change; whatever tension converts experienced because of their decision to join Soka Gakkai was therefore minimized.

In sum, this analysis of the development of SGI-USA demonstrates that both supply-side and demand-side conditions were favorable for the development of Soka Gakkai. However, over and beyond these conditions, largely outside the control of SGI, one must also consider the strategies instituted by organizational leaders. Soka Gakkai played the market well.

Just as Soka Gakkai's successes partly stem from internal processes, therefore, so will the challenges yet to be faced: (1)

those challenges associated with the schism with the Nichiren Shoshu priesthood, and (2) pressure by American converts to further Americanize the organization.

Absence of a Clergy

President Ikeda has served as the movement's primary spiritual leader since 1960, and his continued presence during and since the schism no doubt minimized the damage of separation from the priesthood. Although Soka Gakkai is not currently lacking in capable administrative leadership, there does not appear at this time to be a clear replacement for Ikeda as a spiritual figure-head. The absence of a clergy is thus likely to be felt more acutely when Ikeda retires from the scene.

Already, Soka Gakkai in the United States and elsewhere appears to be shifting its efforts from an exclusive focus on promoting Nichiren Buddhism to include less sectarian efforts for social reform. Soka Gakkai can rightly celebrate this "opening up" of the organization, as Ikeda has described it. Such Soka Gakkai-sponsored affiliate organizations as the Boston Research Center for the Twenty-First Century, Soka University in Tokyo and Los Angeles, and the Min-On Concert Association in Japan are attracting participants from outside the ranks of Soka Gakkai members, establishing identities independent of Soka Gakkai. However, where Soka Gakkai itself is concerned, these efforts represent a drain of resources with very little payoff in terms of promoting Buddhism, which is, presumably, Soka Gakkai's primary goal. If the Soka Gakkai is to avoid becoming largely a peace, culture, and education movement, with its Buddhist foundation increasingly in the background, it will eventually have to find some way to revitalize its spiritual center. To do this, Soka Gakkai may have to develop a clergy of its own. It could be that the current role of "ministers of ceremony" represents the first step toward the development of a Soka Gakkai clergy.

Pressures for Internal Reform

In Chapter 4, we described how SGI-USA has adopted a policy of Americanization, reforming itself to better fit the American religious environment. Despite these efforts, tensions remain over the way the organization is run. In our follow-up interviews, several currently active members raised criticisms about the leadership of the organization. Sometimes, leaders come across as authoritarian, pushing their own agenda without respect for the desires of the members. Many who raised these criticisms thought of this quality as a residue of the Japanese organizational style on which SGI-USA was originally modeled and acknowledged that, especially since Ikeda's visit to the United States in 1990, there has been an attempt to resolve this problem. Therefore, the tension that these members expressed does not indicate a crisis, but it is a problem that must be addressed. These disgruntled members are probably correct in perceiving that such tension is a product of a Japanese leadership style meeting an American constituency. Americans coming out of mainstream American religious denominations are accustomed to the "congregational" model of religious organization, which gives members a great deal of control over the way things are done in their local organization. As first-generation Japanese immigrants are replaced by second-generation Japanese Americans and American converts, there will be increasing pressure by members for more local autonomy. There is every reason to believe, however, that SGI-USA will rise to this challenge. We have already seen how SGI-USA has moved toward the congregational form, and with President Ikeda's sanction and more non-Japanese Americans entering positions of leadership, this trend will probably continue.

An open religious market, a growing demand for religion that speaks to certain experiences of life in a changing society, and sound strategies on the part of Soka Gakkai leaders have secured a place for Soka Gakkai in America. Depending on how SGI-USA deals with the challenge of revitalizing its religious center, however, it is likely that the organization ten years from now will look as different from the organization today as the present organization looks compared to SGI-USA in the 1960s. One way or another, there is reason to believe that Soka Gakkai will be a continuing presence in the American religious landscape.

About this study

A FTER the Executive Director of the Boston Research Center concluded that a study of SGI-USA members was in order, she invited Phillip Hammond to submit a proposal for a survey of its membership. In the summer of 1996 a grant of $24,000 was made to the Institute for Social, Behavioral, and Economic Research, based on the campus of the University of California, Santa Barbara. Two supplemental grants of $2,000 each were subsequently made.

All of this money was spent in two ways: (1) to pay for the costs of the mail questionnaire (printing, mailing, sending reminder letters), and (2) to pay for assistants (two graduate student researchers—David Machacek and Kerry Mitchell—and clerical help). As Principal Investigator, Hammond requested no stipend and received none. Moreover, to insure the independence of the study from those who financed it, all parties agreed that the authors had complete control over what went into the questionnaire as well as what went into this volume.

Of course, the authors consulted with SGI-USA members. For one thing, SGI in America is organized into territorial units, but its membership lists are out of date, especially as the relevant unit increases in geographic and numerical size from the group, through district, chapter, headquarters, region, and finally area, of which there are nineteen in the USA. The only feasible way we had of drawing a random sample of "members" of SGI-USA was to use the subscription lists for the four publications produced and/or distributed by the SGI-USA national headquarters in Santa Monica, California. This meant gaining the cooperation of those SGI-USA leaders, which turned out to be very easy and cordial.

After learning how many subscribers (to one or more of the four publications) lived in each of the regions, we asked that a number of names and addresses be randomly drawn from each region proportional to that region's percentage of the total subscribers' list. Thus, for example, because the Atlanta region (most of the Southeast except Florida) contained 4.3 percent of all subscribers, we asked that 4.3 percent of the sampled names be drawn from that region. Our budget for the mail questionnaire could pay for printing and mailing costs for nearly 1,200 respondents, so it was simple to calculate that the Atlanta region should contribute about 52 names (4.3 percent of 1,200). In all, we ended up with a master list of 1,185 persons in our sample.

Much of the time from September 1996 through March 1997 was spent designing the questionnaire. We had the assistance of many SGI-USA members, who agreed to pre-test our instrument to uncover points of ambiguity and then helped us word and reword certain items. A second pre-test involved a half-dozen or so leaders at the Santa Monica headquarters, who not only pointed out further clarifications but also asked if the questionnaire might include items regarding members' evaluation of SGI publications and its study materials. Of course, we agreed to that request. At no time were we asked to eliminate anything that we had included in the questionnaire.

In April 1997, 1,185 persons were mailed questionnaires. Of this number, some names were removed from the list after they told us they were no longer members or had never been members (some had been given SGI subscriptions by friends in hopes of converting them). Even more names were removed because they could not be found at the address provided and were presumed by the Santa Monica headquarters no longer to be members. All told, we "lost" 104 of the original number. Of the remaining 1,081, we received completed questionnaires from 214 (20 percent) during the first four weeks. A reminder letter, plus an appeal in the form of a news item in SGI-USA's weekly newspaper (*World Tribune*), yielded another 111 questionnaires (10 percent) during the next six weeks. Finally, on June 1 1997, we mailed another appeal with a postcard enclosed. Respondents could use that card (1) to indicate their willingness to complete a questionnaire if we sent another copy, which 76 persons did, or (2) to tell us just three things about themselves (their ethnicity, date of first involvement in SGI, and whether in the past year their SGI involvement had increased, decreased, or remained about the same). Fifty-four persons chose this second option, and we discuss them in Appendix B, where we assess the representativeness of our respondents.

We ceased the collection at the end of August, having received 401 completed questionnaires, for a response rate of 37 percent. While not as high as we had hoped, in certain respects the 401 are known to be representative of the randomly drawn 1,081. In certain other respects the 401 may *not* represent the 1,081. In brief, the 401 are representative in terms of region, gender, and length of membership in SGI, and they are not representative in that the 401 over-represent members who are more involved in SGI. The evidence is not as clear-cut regarding ethnicity, but Asian Americans may be under-represented. These similarities and differences are discussed further in Appendix B.

In retrospect, we erred in creating a questionnaire that was too long. Pre-testers told us they averaged more than one hour in filling it out, but because they did not complain, finding the exercise interesting, we naively assumed that SGI members generally would be interested in the task. Alas, while many obviously were, many more were not.

With 401 completed questionnaires we were at least able to conduct the analysis reported in this volume. We are mindful that, with a sample biased in favor of more involved, and possibly non-Asian, members, to whatever degree we misrepresent SGI-USA *now*, we probably do so in the direction that SGI-USA is *going*. That is to say, the proportion of SGI-USA members who are Asian American has declined during the past four decades, and, while still well represented, they will probably decline further in proportion if not in number. A second point is perhaps more obvious: all organizations are going to be more reflective of their more involved members. A certain "neatness" might have been gained if our sample contained equal proportions of the very involved and less involved, but since it is the character and shape of SGI-USA that we want to understand, we probably get a more—not less—accurate picture by the over-representation of the more involved.

Analysis of the returned questionnaires began after Labor Day 1997 and continued through spring of 1998. The advance contract with Oxford University Press set October 1998 as the date to deliver our book manuscript. We met that deadline with little difficulty.

The Representativeness of the Respondents

BECAUSE surveys are unable to question everyone, survey researchers have developed methods of sampling populations, and much is known about how reliably a sample reflects the universe from which it is drawn. For example, a carefully drawn sample of 1,500 adult Americans will—with 95 percent certainty, and within about three percentage points—accurately mirror the entire adult American population. Thus, suppose for some reason we wanted to know how many Americans wear corrective eyeglasses. We take care to sample 1,500 randomly selected people and learn that 600 of them wear such glasses. A realistic answer to our question would be that, with 95 percent certainty, in the entire population the proportion wearing corrective glasses can be estimated to be in the range of 37 percent to 43 percent. That is to say, 600 is 40 percent of 1,500, and the margin of error is plus or minus 3 percent. Any increase in the sample size will increase the certainty of the estimate, and it will also reduce the margin of error. Thus the bigger the sample the better, but the gain that comes with increased size will seldom be judged to be worth the added costs.

We are confident that the method we used to draw our sample of SGI-USA members yielded a truly random list of names. Since we could not compel people on that list to respond, however, and since we got responses from only 37 percent of the sample, some analysis is required to assess how closely the respondents we did hear from represent the entire sample. We have three ways of addressing this issue:

Method 1

We know some things about even our non-respondents from the list of names itself. We know, for instance, in which region they live, and we can come very close, by knowing their names, to estimating their gender and whether they are of Asian ethnicity. On these three counts, how do our respondents compare with the sample?

A very high correlation exists between the size of the SGI membership in the fifteen regions and the number of returned questionnaires from those areas. The three largest regions are Los Angeles, New York, and San Francisco, in that order. The greatest number of questionnaires were returned from Los Angeles, San Francisco, and New York, in that order. The five smallest regions behaved similarly: lowest in SGI membership are the Midwest, San Diego, Boston, Miami, and Philadelphia, in that order, while the lowest in returned questionnaires were San Diego, the Midwest, Miami, Boston, and Philadelphia. We estimate, therefore, that no regional bias exists in our group of 401 respondents.

What about gender and ethnicity? The sample of names included 31 percent judged to be male, and 25 percent judged to be Asian; among respondents these percentages were 32 percent and 23 percent. These differences are too small to allow any charge of unrepresentativeness, so on these characteristics also, we estimate no gender or ethnic bias in our 401 respondents, at least by the first method of evaluation.

Method 2

Two months after the questionnaires were first mailed, we sent a letter to persons from whom we had not heard. We offered to send a second copy of the questions if they so requested on the enclosed postcard, but for those who were not going to do that, we asked that they at least answer the three questions printed on that postcard and send it back. Fifty-four did so. The three questions asked were: (1) when they first got involved in SGI, (2) whether their involvement now, as compared with a year before, is greater, less, or the same, and (3) their ethnicity. Table 44 shows the answers we received from these 54 people compared with the answers the 401 respondents gave.

We, of course, do not know how representative of all non-respondents the 54 postcard senders are, but some very reasonable

Table 44. Non-respondents vs. respondents (%)

	54 Postcards	Respondents
Date of first involvement:		
Before 1970	23	22
In the 1970s	28	31
In the 1980s	36	37
Since 1990	13	11
Ethnicity:		
Asian	48	27
Black	17	17
Hispanic	12	7
White	23	49
Involvement now as compared to a year ago:		
More	19	44
Less	35	6
About the same	46	50

inferences can be drawn from the above comparisons: (1) Non-respondents and respondents do not differ in their years of involvement; old-timers and newcomers are found in equal proportion in both populations.(2) Unlike our estimate regarding ethnicity using Method 1, Method 2 suggests that non-respondents are over-represented by Asians, which means that Caucasians are over-represented among our respondents. Black SGI-USA members returned the questionnaires in exact proportion to their percent of SGI membership, though Hispanics may be under-represented among all respondents. (3) Finally, Method 2 reveals that failure to return questionnaires indicates—among other things—a declining involvement in SGI. While for both postcard senders and respondents the modal answer (to the question about current involvement compared to a year ago) is "About the same," the postcard senders were six times more likely than respondents to say "Less," and respondents were two-and-a-half times more likely than postcard senders to say "More." A caveat is in order here because the question asked in the questionnaire differed slightly from the question asked on the postcard. Instead of inquiring about "a year ago" (as on the postcard), the questionnaire asked respondents if they expected in the future to be spending more time, less time, or about the same time in SGI activities. This wording change does not invalidate the very sensible inference that people in the process of becoming less involved in an organization will be less inclined to respond to an appeal from that organization, and correlatively, people very involved and expecting to get even more involved will be more inclined to respond to that appeal. .

What about the contradictory evidence regarding Asian ethnicity? Two things might be said by way of reconciling the different findings. First, we got letters from a handful of Japanese American members telling us that their command of English was not great enough to understand our questions. Indeed, some of that handful had a friend or relative write us that letter on their behalf. On that basis we expected an under-representation of (especially) Japanese-speaking respondents since we knew the SGI membership contained many such persons, for whom SGI supplies two Japanese language publications.

Second, we classified people as Asian based on the names on the sample list, and we may have erred enough times to cause our estimate in Method 1 to yield misleading results.

Method 3

A third method of inferring the characteristics of people who did not return questionnaires requires a not unreasonable assumption: people who responded only after repeated appeals, as compared with those who responded early, differ in ways that people who *never* responded differ from those who *did respond*. We coded the date each questionnaire was received, so we can compare early respondents and late respondents on any item in the questionnaire, and thus—by making that assumption—estimate some things about non-respondents.

Some further evidence suggesting Asians are under-represented among our respondents is to be found on this basis. In the first four weeks after questionnaires started arriving, 46 percent were received from persons stating they are Caucasian, and 20 percent were received from persons stating they are Asian. In subsequent weeks, these proportions changed to 37 percent Caucasian and 28 percent Asian. Put another way, a majority of Caucasians (98 of 160, or 61 percent) responded in the early weeks, while a majority of Asians (48 of 90, or 53 percent) responded in the later weeks.

Another interesting hint is this: by far the largest proportion of Asian SGI-USA members is found in the Hawaii region. Hawaii had one of the lowest rates of returned questionnaires in weeks 1–4, dropped even lower in weeks 5–10, and had nearly the highest rate of return in the final six weeks. In other words, Hawaii was among the least co-operative regions until our efforts finally elicited 19 responses. It ended up with the second-lowest response rate (24 percent). Although the numbers are small they may be significant: in the first four weeks, 5 of 8 returns (63 percent) were from Asians; in subsequent weeks, 10 of 11 returns (91 percent) were from Asians.

Method 3 also yields some confirmation that respondents are more involved in SGI activities than are non-respondents. For example, chanting—the chief ritual of SGI—is supposed to be done every morning and evening, and 59 percent of the respondents report that they accomplish this goal. The other 41 percent do not, however, and it is probably significant that early respondents have a higher chanting average (6.28 times per week) than later respondents (5.6 times per week).

SGI is a multi-layered organization, with a layer at the international level and lower layers descending to what is called the "group." Respondents who returned questionnaires early report being better informed about all levels than do late returners, and they also express greater satisfaction with leadership at all levels, especially at the group level. The exception is at the international level, where there is overwhelming satisfaction at each return time period and virtually no dissatisfaction.

All other involvement measures and demographic items of information showed no systematic differences as we looked across early, middle, and late returns. Any of these latter differences were purely random, we have to assume.

Can a conclusion be drawn, therefore, as to the representativeness of our respondents relative to the randomly drawn sample? The answer is probably "yes," and it is the answer with which Appendix A concluded—that our study may under-represent Asian SGI-USA members, just as it does the less involved. However, these two attributes are related. Japanese members are twice as likely as all other members to be in the "core" group, and only half as likely to be "marginal." Just as language problems may have decreased the response rate of Japanese members, then, so may their higher rate of involvement increase it. As we said in Appendix A, however, the degree to which we misrepresent SGI-USA *now* probably represents the direction SGI-USA is *going*.

The Survey Instrument

SGI-USA Membership Survey

The following questions ask about your opinions, experiences, and activities.

- Please answer each question as honestly and completely as possible.
- Please take your time, and read each question carefully.
- This is not a test! There are no right or wrong answers.

Section A: First, we would like to ask about your experiences in SGI.

1. At what date did you first encounter SGI-USA (NSA)? _____

2. At what date did you first start chanting? _____

3. Are you now a member?
   - ☐ Yes *If yes*—when did you actually join? _____
   - ☐ No   *If no*—please use the enclosed card to tell us that. Provide your name and address. You may then throw away this questionnaire.

4. How did you first encounter SGI-USA (NSA)? (*Mark one.*)
   - ☐ Through my spouse (or future spouse)
   - ☐ Through a member of my family
   - ☐ Through a work colleague
   - ☐ Through a friend

- ☐ Through a casual acquaintance
- ☐ At an exhibition or concert
- ☐ By literature or publicity
- ☐ Some other means. Please specify: _____

5. What was your first reaction to what you observed? (*Mark one.*)
   - ☐ Immediate enthusiasm for SGI
   - ☐ Some interest in SGI
   - ☐ A reluctance to learn more
   - ☐ Real skepticism
   - ☐ Other. What? _____

6. If you first encountered SGI-USA (NSA) through an individual,

   A. Did this person invite   ☐ I initiated   ☐ S/he initiated
   you to a meeting, or   contact   contact
   did you initiate contact?

   B. Was that individual   ☐ Yes   ☐ No
   Japanese?

   C. Was that individual   ☐ Male   ☐ Female
   male or female?

7. Which *one* of these statements best describes how you got involved in SGI-USA (NSA)?
   - ☐ I had heard and read enough about SGI to know that I wanted to get involved.
   - ☐ I got acquainted with one or more SGI members who impressed me so much that I decided to get involved.
   - ☐ Almost by chance, I was invited to an SGI meeting, was immediately impressed, and got involved.
   - ☐ I got involved reluctantly to please someone else, but then I saw what chanting could do, so I got involved.
   - ☐ I was curious, so I tried practicing, liked the results, and got involved.
   - ☐ Other. Please describe: _____

8. Apart from the teachings, can you say what originally attracted you to SGI-USA (NSA)?

9. Is the original attraction still the most significant aspect of SGI-USA for you?
   - ☐ Yes

☐ No   *If no*—what is NOW the most attractive feature of the organization?

10. In what religious tradition were you raised? *(If Protestant, please indicate the specific denomination.)*

11. Apart from the religion in which you were raised, did you have any other religious preferences before joining SGI-USA?
☐ Yes
☐ No

If yes—Please list them in order from then to now, and indicate the approximate dates. (*Example*—Roman Catholic, from 1977 to 1982.)

A.
B.
C.
D.

12. Whether or not you belonged to some other faith, would you say that you were a religious person before joining SGI-USA (NSA)? (*Mark one.*)
☐ Yes, I was very religious.
☐ I was not very religious, but I was aware of spiritual matters.
☐ No, I was not very concerned about religion or spirituality at that time.
☐ Other. Please describe: _____

13. We would like to know more about your life experiences before joining SGI-USA (NSA). Which of the following statements best describe your life prior to your first encounter with SGI-USA (NSA)? (*Mark as many as apply.*)
☐ I felt like I was at a turning point in my life.
☐ I was very interested in Eastern religion and philosophy.
☐ I was looking for something new and exciting to do with my life.
☐ I felt a strong need for guidance and direction in my life.
☐ I was feeling lonely at that time.
☐ I wanted more out of life than I was getting.
☐ I was experiencing serious problems. Please describe: _____
☐ I was living a satisfying life with only ordinary problems.

☐ Other. Please describe: _____

14. (*Mark as many as apply.*) At the time of your first encounter with SGI-USA (NSA):

A.	Were you employed full-time?	☐ Yes	☐ No
B.	Were you employed part-time?	☐ Yes	☐ No
C.	Were you a full-time student?	☐ Yes	☐ No
D.	Were you unemployed?	☐ Yes	☐ No
E.	Were you married, or living with a partner?	☐ Yes	☐ No
F.	Were you living in the same geographic area as your parents or siblings?	☐ Yes	☐ No
G.	Were you spiritually satisfied?	☐ Yes	☐ No
H.	Had you undertaken any sort of psychotherapy?	☐ Yes	☐ No
I.	Had you ever traveled outside the US?	☐ Yes	☐ No
J.	Had you read much about non-Western cultures?	☐ Yes	☐ No

15. Before becoming acquainted with SGI-USA (NSA) had you encountered:

A.	Any other form of Buddhism?	☐ Yes	☐ No
	If yes—which? _____		
B.	Any other form of Eastern religion?	☐ Yes	☐ No
	If yes—which? _____		

16. Before becoming acquainted with SGI-USA (NSA) had you any particular interest in Japan or things Japanese?

☐ Yes
☐ No

If yes—please indicate the form(s) which that interest took by marking the appropriate category(ies).

☐ Language
☐ Literature
☐ Graphic Arts
☐ Films
☐ Martial Arts
☐ Cuisine
☐ Other. Please specify: _____

17. Are any of your close relatives members of SGI-USA (NSA)?

- ☐ Yes
- ☐ No

If yes—please mark the relevant category(ies), and for each category marked, indicate who joined first.

	I joined first	He/she/they joined first
☐ Wife/Husband (Girl/Boy Friend)	1	2
☐ Father	1	2
☐ Mother	1	2
☐ Brother(s)/Sister(s)	1	2
☐ Father-in-law	1	2
☐ Mother-in-law	1	2
☐ Brother(s)/Sister(s)-in-law	1	2
☐ Other relatives	1	2

18. If you have children over 18 years of age, are any of them members of SGI-USA (NSA)? ☐ Yes ☐ No

If yes—please indicate how many out of how many: ____ out of ____

19. Do you find it possible to volunteer your time for SGI-USA?

- ☐ Yes   *If yes*—in what capacity?
- ☐ No

20. Do you expect that you will be spending more time or less time volunteering for the organization in the future, or will it stay about the same?

- ☐ More time
- ☐ About the same
- ☐ Less time

21. Please tell us if you have held, now hold, or would be willing to hold a leadership position at any of these levels in SGI:

		Never held	Have held	Now hold	Willing to hold
A.	Group	1	2	3	4
B.	District	1	2	3	4
C.	Chapter	1	2	3	4
D.	Headquarters	1	2	3	4

E.	Area	1	2	3	4
F.	Region	1	2	3	4

22. How satisfied are you with the opportunities for assuming leadership positions in SGI-USA?
- ☐ Very satisfied
- ☐ Somewhat satisfied
- ☐ Somewhat dissatisfied
- ☐ Very dissatisfied

23. How many of your close friends are members of SGI-USA (NSA)? Please indicate the number; out of how many close friends: ___ out of _____

24. Do you find it possible to practice every   ☐ Yes   ☐ No morning and evening without fail?

    If no—please estimate how many times a week you normally practice: _____

25. What would you say have been the principal benefits to you from practicing?

26. Have you ever chanted to realize a particular goal or goals?
- ☐ Yes   *If yes*—please give some examples:
- ☐ No

27. Were the goals for which you chanted realized?
- ☐ Yes   *If yes*—in what way?
- ☐ No

28. Have you ever chanted for a goal that was not realized?
- ☐ Yes
- ☐ No (Go to Q. 29)

    28a. *If yes*—what was it?

    28b. From the list below, mark the one reason that you believe *best* explains why this goal was not realized:
- ☐ The goal was incompatible with lifelong happiness/ Buddhahood.
- ☐ Chanting doesn't work for some goals.
- ☐ I probably need to go through my human revolution before I'll achieve that goal.
- ☐ I wasn't practicing correctly.

☐   Other reasons. Please explain: _____

28c. Will you continue to chant for   ☐   Yes   ☐   No
this goal?

29. Have you experienced any difficulties or negative reactions from relatives and friends because you belong to SGI-USA (NSA)?
☐   Yes   *If yes*—by whom? and in what circumstances?
☐   No

30. How important has the support of other SGI members been to your practice, personally?
☐   Not very important. I would chant anyway.
☐   Somewhat important.
☐   Very important. I would probably chant less often if not for their support.

31. It has been said that SGI-USA has moved away from active, aggressive *shakubuku* toward a more passive, show-by-example recruitment method:

A. Do you think this is the case?   ☐   Yes, definitely
                                            ☐   Yes , somewhat
                                            ☐   No

B. If yes—do you approve of this change?   ☐   Yes, definitely
                                            ☐   Yes, somewhat
                                            ☐   No

32. Have you, yourself, been active in introducing others into SGI-USA?
☐   Yes, very active
☐   Yes, somewhat
☐   No (Go to Q. 33)

32a. *If yes*—how many persons have you introduced?
☐   One
☐   Two–four
☐   Five–fifteen
☐   Sixteen or more

32b. What has happened with those you introduced? Are they still active in SGI-USA?
☐   All remain active.

☐ Most remain active.
☐ Less than half remain active.
☐ All have dropped out.

33. As you know, SGI and Nichiren Shoshu split in 1991. How do you feel about that split personally?
☐ SGI-USA is better off since the split.
☐ SGI-USA was harmed by the split.
☐ The split made little difference in SGI-USA.

34. In general, how much do events that happen with SGI in Japan influence:

	Not at all	Some	Quite a lot
A. Your own practice, personally?	1	2	3
B. Your local group?	1	2	3
C. SGI in the United States?	1	2	3

35. Are you, yourself connected with the Nichiren Shoshu temple?
☐ Yes
☐ No

If yes—how are you connected? ☐ I'm a member.
☐ I attend Temple meetings.
☐ Through friends/family.
☐ I feel an emotional connection.

35B. Do you know of former NSA members in America who chose to remain connected to the Nichiren Shoshu temple rather than become SGI-USA members?
☐ No, I don't know of any.
☐ Yes, I know just a handful.
☐ Yes, I know of dozens (or more).

If yes—do you know why these people chose to remain connected to the temple?

36. How well do you keep informed about SGI:

	Very well	Pretty well	Some	Not much
A. Internationally?	1	2	3	4
B. In the US?	1	2	3	4

C. In your Territory?	1	2	3	4
D. In your District?	1	2	3	4
E. In your Group?	1	2	3	4

37. In general, are you satisfied with the leadership of SGI-USA:

	Satisfied	Neutral	Dissatisfied
A. Internationally?	1	2	3
B. In the US?	1	2	3
C. In your Territory?	1	2	3
D. In your District?	1	2	3
E. In your Group?	1	2	3

38. About how many hours *per week* do you spend:

	None	1 hour	2–3 hours	4–10 hours	11+ hours
A. Reading the *World Tribune*?	0	1	2	3	4
B. Reading *Seikyo Times* (*Living Buddhism*)?	0	1	2	3	4
C. Attending SGI-USA gatherings?	0	1	2	3	4
D. Talking about SGI with non-members?	0	1	2	3	4
E. Reading *Seikyo Shimbun*?	0	1	2	3	4
F. Reading *Daibyaku Renge*?	0	1	2	3	4

39. How familiar are you with the SGI-USA Course of Study materials?
- ☐ Very familiar—I use them regularly.
- ☐ Somewhat familiar—I use them sometimes.
- ☐ I'm aware of them, but have not used them.
- ☐ I'm not really aware of them.

If you are familiar with these materials—do you think they need to be improved?
- ☐ Yes, definitely.
- ☐ Yes, probably.
- ☐ No. They are fine now.

40. Do you think the *World Tribune* (*Living Buddhism*) needs to be improved?
- ☐ Yes, definitely.

☐ Yes, probably.

☐ No. It is fine now.

If yes—what specifically needs improvement?

41. In your opinion, how realistic is the goal of bringing about world peace?

☐ Very realistic (1)

☐ Pretty realistic (2)

☐ Not very realistic (3)

☐ Not at all realistic

If you answered 1, 2, or 3—What do you think will be SGI's contribution to whatever is accomplished in the area of world peace? (*Mark one*)

☐ SGI's contribution is essential, but so are other efforts.

☐ SGI's contribution is important, but other contributions are probably more important.

☐ SGI's contribution is not very important.

42. Do you believe that chanting alone is sufficient to bring about world peace?

☐ Yes

☐ No

43. Besides chanting, what else are you, yourself, doing (or have you done in the past) to bring about the goal of world peace?

44. Besides chanting, what else is SGI doing as an organization to bring about the goal of world peace?

45. Do you think that, by cooperating with such other organized religions as Christianity, Judaism, or Islam in promoting world peace, SGI will compromise its commitment to the teachings of Nichiren?

☐ Yes, definitely

☐ Yes, probably

☐ Probably not

☐ Definitely not

46. What about cooperating with other Buddhist groups? Would that compromise SGI's commitment to the teachings of Nichiren?

☐ Yes, definitely

☐ Yes, probably

☐ Probably not

☐   Definitely not

47. How likely is it that you will drop out of SGI-USA someday?
    ☐   I'll never stop chanting or going to group meetings.
    ☐   It's very unlikely that I will stop chanting or going to group meetings.
    ☐   I'll never stop chanting, though I might cut down on my attendance at meetings.
    ☐   There is a chance that I will drop out.

Section B: Here are some questions about your social experiences and opinions about contemporary issues in the United States.

48. We'd like to know about some leisure or recreational activities that you do during your free time. For *each* activity listed please indicate whether or not it is something you have done in the past twelve months.

A	Attended an amateur or professional sports event.	☐	Yes	☐	No
B.	Visited an art museum or gallery.	☐	Yes	☐	No
C.	Made art or craft objects such as pottery, woodworking, quilts, or paintings.	☐	Yes	☐	No
D.	Gone to an auto, stock car, or motorcycle race.	☐	Yes	☐	No
E.	Gone camping, hiking, or canoeing.	☐	Yes	☐	No
F.	Grown vegetables, flowers, or shrubs in a garden.	☐	Yes	☐	No
G.	Gone to a live ballet or dance performance, not including school performances.	☐	Yes	☐	No
H.	Gone to a classical music or opera performance, not including school performances.	☐	Yes	☐	No
I.	Gone hunting or fishing.	☐	Yes	☐	No
J.	Taken part in a music, dance, or theatrical performance.	☐	Yes	☐	No
K.	Participated in any sports activity such as softball, basketball, swimming, golf, bowling, skiing, or tennis.	☐	Yes	☐	No

L. Gone out to see a movie in a theater. ☐ Yes ☐ No
M. Recorded a TV program so you could ☐ Yes ☐ No
    watch it later.
N. Played a musical instrument such as a ☐ Yes ☐ No
    piano, guitar, or violin.

49. (*Mark one answer for each.*) Do you think it proper for religious bodies to speak out on:

A.	Disarmament	☐	Yes ☐ No
B.	Abortion	☐	Yes ☐ No
C.	Third World problems	☐	Yes ☐ No
D.	Extra-marital affairs	☐	Yes ☐ No
E.	Unemployment	☐	Yes ☐ No
F.	Racial discrimination	☐	Yes ☐ No
G.	Euthanasia	☐	Yes ☐ No
H.	Homosexuality	☐	Yes ☐ No
I.	Ecology and environment	☐	Yes ☐ No
J.	Government policy	☐	Yes ☐ No

50. Now we would like to know something about the groups and organizations to which you belong. Here is a list of various kinds of organizations. Please indicate whether or not you are a member of *each* type:

A.	Fraternal groups	☐	Yes ☐ No
B.	Non-SGI service clubs	☐	Yes ☐ No
C.	Veterans' groups	☐	Yes ☐ No
D.	Political clubs	☐	Yes ☐ No
E.	Labor unions	☐	Yes ☐ No
F.	Sports clubs	☐	Yes ☐ No
G.	Youth groups	☐	Yes ☐ No
H.	School service clubs	☐	Yes ☐ No
I.	Hobby or garden clubs	☐	Yes ☐ No
J.	School fraternities or sororities	☐	Yes ☐ No
K.	Nationality or ethnicity groups	☐	Yes ☐ No
L.	Farm organizations	☐	Yes ☐ No
M.	Literary, art, discussion, or study groups	☐	Yes ☐ No
N.	Professional or academic societies	☐	Yes ☐ No

51. Below is a list of some things that different people value. Some people say these things are very important to them. Other people say

they are not so important. How important is *each* of these things to you personally?

		Very Important	Somewhat Important	Not Very Important	Not at all Important
A.	Being financially secure.	1	2	3	4
B.	Being married.	1	2	3	4
C.	Having children.	1	2	3	4
D.	Having faith.	1	2	3	4
E.	Having nice things.	1	2	3	4
F.	Being cultured.	1	2	3	4
G.	Having a fulfilling job.	1	2	3	4
H.	Being self-sufficient and not having to depend on others.	1	2	3	4
I.	Having leisure time.	1	2	3	4
J.	Staying informed politically.	1	2	3	4

52. Some people say there's too much cynicism in America, that people should be actively involved in making things better. What do you think? (*Mark one.*)
- ☐ Agree strongly.
- ☐ Agree somewhat.
- ☐ Not sure. Sometimes I agree, sometimes I disagree.
- ☐ Disagree. There's good reason to be cynical.

53. Some people think Americans are too concerned about material possessions and should be less worldly. How do you feel about that? (*Mark one.*)
- ☐ Agree strongly.
- ☐ Agree somewhat.
- ☐ Not sure. It depends.
- ☐ Disagree. There's nothing wrong with desiring material things.

54. Please indicate how strongly you agree or disagree with *each* of the following statements:

		Agree strongly	Agree	Neither	Disagree	Disagree strongly
A.	All in all, family life suffers when the woman has a full-time job.	1	2	3	4	5

B.	A woman and her family will be happier if she goes out to work.	1	2	3	4	5
C.	A job is alright, but what most women really want is a home and children.	1	2	3	4	5
D.	Having a job is the best way for a woman to be an independent person.	1	2	3	4	5
E.	Both the husband and the wife should contribute to the household income.	1	2	3	4	5
F.	A husband's job is to earn money; a wife's job is to look after the home and family.	1	2	3	4	5

55. Why are there people in this country who live in need? Here are some possible reasons. Please indicate for *each* reason whether you think it is very important, somewhat important, or not important in explaining why some people are poor in this country.

		Very important	Somewhat important	Not important
A.	Failure of society to provide good schools for many Americans.	1	2	3
B.	Loose morals and drunkenness.	1	2	3
C.	Failure of industry to provide enough jobs.	1	2	3
D.	Lack of effort by the poor themselves.	1	2	3

56. Would you say that most of the time people try to be helpful, or that they are mostly just looking out for themselves?
   ☐   People try to be helpful.
   ☐   People just look out for themselves.

57. Do you think most people would try to take advantage of you if they got a chance, or would they try to be fair?
   ☐   People will take advantage of you.
   ☐   People try to be fair.

58. Generally speaking, would you say that most people can be trusted or that you can't be too careful in dealing with people?
- ☐ Most people can be trusted.
- ☐ You can't be too careful.

59. Now, we'd like to know how you would respond to a couple of common decisions. For each situation, please indicate how you would *most likely* respond.

59a. Let's say you were in a store and saw something you really wanted, but you didn't have enough cash to buy it. Would you be more likely to:
- ☐ Buy it on credit.
- ☐ Save up your money and return to buy it later.

59b. Suppose you were shopping for a new appliance. You need it soon, but you want to make a careful decision. Would you be more likely to spend your time shopping around for the best price, or researching the reliability and performance of the products?
- ☐ Shopping for the best price.
- ☐ Researching reliability and performance.

60. What should be the aims of this country for the next ten years? Below are listed some goals to which some people give priority. Would you please say which one of these you yourself consider the most important? And which would be the second most important? (*Write "1" next to your first choice, and write "2" next to your second choice.*)
- _____ Maintaining a high level of economic growth.
- _____ Making sure the country has strong defense forces.
- _____ Seeing that people have more say about how things are done at their jobs and in their communities.
- _____ Trying to make our cities and countryside more beautiful.

61. If you had to choose, which of the things on the list below would you say is most important? Which would you consider second most important? (*Write "1" next to your first choice, and write "2" next to your second choice.*)
- _____ Maintaining order in the nation.
- _____ Giving people more say in important government decisions.

_____ Fighting rising prices.

_____ Protecting freedom of speech.

62. Here is another list. In your opinion, which one of these is most important? And what would be the next most important? (*Write "1" next to your first choice, and write "2" next to your second choice.*)

_____ A stable economy.

_____ Progress towards a less impersonal and more humane society.

_____ Progress towards a society in which ideas count more than money.

_____ The fight against crime.

63. For *each* of the following statements, please indicate how strongly you agree or disagree.

		Agree strongly	Agree	Neither	Disagree	Disagree strongly
A.	You have to take care of yourself first, and if you have any energy left over, then help other people.	1	2	3	4	5
B.	People should be allowed to accumulate as much wealth as they can even if some make millions while others live in poverty.	1	2	3	4	5

64. Please indicate which *one* of these statements comes closest to your views.

☐ Nature is sacred because it is created by God.

☐ Nature is spiritual or sacred in itself.

☐ Nature is important, but not spiritual or sacred.

☐ Don't know/Can't choose.

65. In political matters, people talk of the "left" (liberal) and the "right" (conservative). Generally speaking where would place your views on this scale? (1 being the most liberal, and 7 being most conservative):

Liberal 1------2------3------4------5------6------7 Conservative

66. Did you vote in the 1996 presidential election? ☐ Yes ☐ No

    66a. *If yes*—for whom did you vote?
        ☐   Bill Clinton
        ☐   Bob Dole
        ☐   Someone else. Please specify: _____

67. Do you regard yourself generally as a Democrat, Republican, Independent, or something else?
    ☐   Democrat
    ☐   Republican
    ☐   Independent
    ☐   Other. Please specify: _____

68. These days, people are saying a lot of different things about the future. Which *one* of the following statements most nearly expresses your own view?
    ☐   I expect human differences and competition of national interests to build toward a major conflict.
    ☐   I expect things to be about the same as they are now.
    ☐   I think that humanity will awaken spiritually and overcome our differences and conflicts.
    ☐   Other. Please describe: _____

69. Here is a list of various changes in our way of life that might take place in the near future. Please say for *each* one, if the change would be a good thing, or a bad thing.

		Good	Bad	Depends
A.	Less emphasis on money and material possessions.	1	2	3
B.	Decrease in the importance of work in our lives.	1	2	3
C.	More emphasis on the development of technology.	1	2	3
D.	Greater emphasis on the development of the individual.	1	2	3
E.	Greater respect for authority.	1	2	3
F.	More emphasis on family life.	1	2	3
G.	A simple and more natural lifestyle.	1	2	3

H. More openness to change in   1   2   3
    society.

70. Please look at this list and tell us how much confidence you have in *each* of these institutions: is it a great deal of confidence; quite a lot; not very much; or none at all?

		A great deal	Quite a lot	Not much	None at all
A.	Organized religion	1	2	3	4
B.	The armed forces	1	2	3	4
C.	The educational system	1	2	3	4
D.	The legal system	1	2	3	4
E.	The news media	1	2	3	4
F.	Unions	1	2	3	4
G.	Congress	1	2	3	4
H.	The Supreme Court	1	2	3	4
I.	The executive branch of the federal government	1	2	3	4
J.	Major corporations	1	2	3	4
K.	Hospitals/Health care	1	2	3	4
L.	The police	1	2	3	4
M.	The social security system	1	2	3	4
N.	United Nations	1	2	3	4

71. The following questions are about your outlook on life. Each item has two contrasting statements on it. Using the scale listed, where would you place your own view? (*1 means you agree completely with the statement on the left; 10 means you agree completely with the statement on the right; or you can choose any number in between.*)

☐ 1   ☐ 2   ☐ 3   ☐ 4   ☐ 5   ☐ 6   ☐ 7   ☐ 8   ☐ 9   ☐ 10

A. One should be cautious about making major changes in life.	You will never achieve much unless you act boldly.

☐ 1   ☐ 2   ☐ 3   ☐ 4   ☐ 5   ☐ 6   ☐ 7   ☐ 8   ☐ 9   ☐ 10

B. Ideas that have stood the test of time are generally best.	New ideas are generally better than old ones.

□ 1	□ 2	□ 3	□ 4	□ 5	□ 6	□ 7	□ 8	□ 9	□ 10

C. When changes occur in my life, I worry about the difficulties they may cause.

When changes occur in my life, I welcome the possibility that something new is beginning.

□ 1	□ 2	□ 3	□ 4	□ 5	□ 6	□ 7	□ 8	□ 9	□ 10

D. I am an extremely independent person.

I rely heavily on others.

□ 1	□ 2	□ 3	□ 4	□ 5	□ 6	□ 7	□ 8	□ 9	□ 10

E. In this world, only the strong survive.

We're all in this together, so it is important to look out for each other.

□ 1	□ 2	□ 3	□ 4	□ 5	□ 6	□ 7	□ 8	□ 9	□ 10

F. The universe is basically friendly if one knows the right things.

The way the universe works is basically an unknowable mystery.

72. Here are some more questions about your outlook on life. Would you tend to agree or disagree with each of the following statements?

		Agree	Disagree	Neither
A.	In spite of what some people say, the lot (situation/ condition) of the average person is getting worse, not better.	1	2	3
B.	It's hardly fair to bring a child into the world with the way things look for the future.	1	2	3
C.	Most public officials (people in public office) are not really interested in the problems of the average person.	1	2	3

73. Please indicate how much you agree or disagree with *each* of the following statements:

		Agree strongly	Agree	Neither	Disagree	Disagree strongly
A.	Overall, modern science does more harm than good.	1	2	3	4	5
B.	People worry too much about human progress harming the environment.	1	2	3	4	5
C.	It is just too difficult for someone like me to do much about the environment.	1	2	3	4	5
D.	I do what is right for the environment, even when it costs more money or takes up more time.	1	2	3	4	5

74. Here are some things that have been said about science. Please indicate whether you tend to agree or disagree with *each* of them.

		Agree	Disagree	Neither
A.	Science will solve our social problems like crime and mental illness.	1	2	3
B.	One trouble with science is that it makes our way of life change too fast.	1	2	3
C.	Scientists always seem to be prying into things that they really ought to stay out of.	1	2	3
D.	One of the bad effects of science is that it breaks down people's ideas of right and wrong.	1	2	3

75. Please consider the following statements and indicate whether you agree strongly, agree somewhat, disagree somewhat, or disagree strongly with *each* statement.

		Agree strongly	Agree	Disagree	Disagree strongly
A.	Right and wrong are not usually a simple matter of black and white; there are many shades of gray.	1	2	3	4
B.	Immoral actions by one person can corrupt society in general.	1	2	3	4
C.	Morality is a personal matter and society should not force everyone to follow one standard.	1	2	3	4

76. There's been a lot of discussion about the way morals and attitudes about sex are changing in this country. Please indicate how you feel about *each* of the following sexual behaviors. Are they always wrong, almost always wrong, wrong only sometimes, or not wrong at all?

		Always wrong	Almost always wrong	Wrong sometimes	Not wrong at all
A.	If a man and woman have sex before marriage?	1	2	3	4
B.	What if they are in their early teens, say 14 to 16 years old?	1	2	3	4
C.	What about a married person having sexual relations with someone other than the marriage partner?	1	2	3	4
D.	What about sexual relations between two adults of the same sex?	1	2	3	4

77. If someone said that individuals should have the chance to enjoy complete sexual freedom without being restricted, would you tend to agree or disagree?
☐   Tend to agree.
☐   Tend to disagree.
☐   Neither/It depends.

78. Do you think the use of marijuana should be made legal or not?
☐   Yes, it should be legal.
☐   No, it should not be legal.

79. Please indicate whether or not you think it should be possible for a pregnant woman to obtain a legal abortion:

A.   If there is a strong chance of a serious   ☐ Yes   ☐ No
defect in the baby?

B.   If she is married and does not want any   ☐ Yes   ☐ No
more children?

C.   If the woman's own health is seriously   ☐ Yes   ☐ No
endangered by the pregnancy?

D.   If the family has a very low income and   ☐ Yes   ☐ No
cannot afford any more children?

E.   If she became pregnant as a result of   ☐ Yes   ☐ No
rape?

F.   If she is not married and does not want   ☐ Yes   ☐ No
to marry the man?

G.   The woman wants it for any reason?   ☐ Yes   ☐ No

80. What do you think will happen as a result of more immigrants coming to this country? Is *each* of these possible results very likely, somewhat likely, not too likely, or not at all likely?

		Very likely	Somewhat likely	Not too likely	Not at all likely
A.	Higher economic growth.	1	2	3	4
B.	Higher unemployment.	1	2	3	4
C.	Making it harder to keep the country united.	1	2	3	4

81. In history classes in high school and college, do the experiences of racial and ethnic minority groups in America receive too much attention now, too little attention, or about the right amount?

☐ Too much attention
☐ Too little attention
☐ About the right amount

82. Do you agree or disagree with *each* of the following statements?

		Agree strongly	Agree	Disagree	Disagree strongly
A.	Life, as experienced by most people, is not what it should be.	1	2	3	4
B.	Most people are like machines, merely reacting to external situations.	1	2	3	4
C.	Happiness cannot be achieved through things external to the self.	1	2	3	4
D.	Happiness can only be achieved through inner, spiritual transformation.	1	2	3	4

83. How often do you read the newspaper, other than the *World Tribune*—every day, a few times a week, once a week, less than once a week, or never?
☐ Every day
☐ A few times a week
☐ Once a week
☐ Less than once a week
☐ Never

84. How often do you use the internet—every day, a few times a week, once a week, less than once a week, or never?
☐ Every day
☐ A few times a week
☐ Once a week
☐ Less than once a week
☐ Never

85. On the average day, about how many hours do you personally watch television?

86. On the average day, about how many hours do you listen to the radio?

87. Think about all of your really close friends—relatives, coworkers, friends from school, friends from SGI, and so forth. How many of them know each other—nearly all of them, most of them, or only a few of them?
  - ☐ Nearly all
  - ☐ Most
  - ☐ Only a few
  - ☐ None

    87a. How many of them live right in your local area?
  - ☐ Nearly all
  - ☐ Most
  - ☐ Only a few
  - ☐ None

88. Now, think about the people in your neighborhood. Are you close to many of them, a few of them, or hardly any of them?
  - ☐ Many
  - ☐ A few
  - ☐ Hardly any
  - ☐ None

Section C: Please take a moment to look back at your responses to questions (48–88) in Section B. Have any of your attitudes changed as a result of your involvement in SGI? If so, please write below the question number and what your response would probably have been before you joined SGI. Do not change any of your original answers on the previous pages.

Section D: Finally, we would like to ask you some questions about yourself. We emphasize that the information you give is confidential and that you will remain anonymous.

89. Please indicate your sex: ☐ Male ☐ Female

90. In what year were you born? _____

91. What is your occupation or profession? _____

    91a. Please specify your actual job: _____

92. Please indicate your current employment status. (*Mark all that apply.*)
   - ☐ Employed full-time
   - ☐ Self-employed
   - ☐ Employed part-time
   - ☐ Housewife not otherwise employed
   - ☐ Retired/Pensioned
   - ☐ Student, in full-time education
   - ☐ Unemployed

93. What is your approximate yearly income?
   - ☐ Less than $10,000
   - ☐ $10,000–20,000
   - ☐ $20,000–30,000
   - ☐ $30,000–40,000
   - ☐ $40,000–50,000
   - ☐ $50,000–60,000
   - ☐ $60,000–70,000
   - ☐ $70,000 or more

94. What is your race/ethnic background? (*If mixed race, please mark "other" and describe.*)
   - ☐ White
   - ☐ Black
   - ☐ Asian/Pacific Islander.
   - ☐ Latino/Hispanic.
   - ☐ Other. Please specify: _____

95. From what country or countries did your ancestors come?

   95a. If you named two or more countries or parts of the world, which one of these do you feel closest to?

   95b. Do you feel closer to other people from the same national background as yourself?
   - ☐ Yes
   - ☐ No

96. Are you currently:
   - ☐ Married?
   - ☐ Living with a partner?
   - ☐ Divorced?

☐ Separated?
☐ Widowed?
☐ Single?
☐ Other? Please specify: _____

97. Have you ever been divorced?   ☐ Yes   ☐ No

98. In what state do you currently reside? _____

99. In what state or country were you born? _____

100. How would you characterize the place where you live?
☐ A rural area
☐ A small town
☐ A medium-sized city
☐ A large city
☐ A suburb of a major city/metropolitan area

101. At what age did you complete full-time education? _____

102. What is the highest level of education you have *completed*?
☐ Grammar school (elementary and junior high)
☐ High school
☐ Some college
☐ Trade school, or junior college
☐ Bachelor's degree
☐ Graduate or professional degree

This section is voluntary.

We would like to conduct a few personal follow-up interviews with respondents to this questionnaire. If you would be willing to participate in a phone conversation with one of the researchers, please write your name, phone number, and the days and times you are most likely to be available.

Name: _____   Phone #: (___) _____

Days of the week and times when it is best to reach you: _____

Thank you

References

NSA Quarterly (Summer 1976).

BELLAH, ROBERT, "Civil Religion in America," *Daedalus*, 96/1 (1967), 1–20.

BRINKERHOFF, M. B., and BURKE, KATHERINE L., "Disaffiliation: Some Notes on 'Falling from the Faith,' " *Sociological Analysis*, 41 (1980), 41–54.

CAPLOVITZ, DAVID, and SHERROW, FRED, *The Religious Dropouts* (Beverly Hills, Calif.: Sage, 1977).

EPPSTEINER, ROBERT, *The Soka Gakkai International: Religious Roots, Early History and Contemporary Development* (Cambridge, Mass.: Soka Gakkai International—USA, 1997).

FINKE, ROGER, and IANNACCONE, LAURENCE, "Supply-Side Explanations for Religious Change," *Annals of the American Academy of Political and Social Science*, 527 (1993), 27–39.

—— and STARK, RODNEY, *The Churching of America, 1776–1990: Winners and Losers in our Religious Economy* (New Brunswick, NJ: Rutgers University Press, 1992).

GUTTMAN, LOUIS, "The Basis for Scalogram Analysis," in S. Stouffer *et al.* (eds.), *Measurement and Prediction* (Princeton: Princeton University Press, 1992).

HAMMOND, PHILLIP E., *Religion and Personal Autonomy: The Third Disestablishment in America* (Columbia, SC: University of South Carolina Press, 1992).

—— *With Liberty for All* (Louisville, Ky.: Westminster John Knox Press, 1998).

HANDY, ROBERT, *A Christian America*, 2nd edn. (New York: Oxford University Press, 1984).

HASHIMOTO, HIDEO, and MCPHERSON, WILLIAM, "Rise and Decline of Sokagakkai: Japan and the United States," *Review of Religious Research*, 17/2 (1976), 82–92.

HURST, JANE, "A Buddhist Reformation in the 20th Century: Causes and Implications of the Conflict between Soka Gakkai and the Nichiren Shoshu Priesthood," Paper presented at the Harvard Buddhist Studies Forum Conference, Harvard University, Cambridge, Mass., May 1997.

HURST, JANE, "The Nichiren Shoshu Soka Gakkai in America: The Ethos of a New Religious Movement," Ph.D. thesis, Temple University, 1980.

IANNACCONE, LAURENCE, "The Consequences of Religious Market Structure," *Rationality and Society*, 3 (1991), 156–77.

—— "Religious Practice: A Human Capital Approach," *Journal for the Scientific Study of Religion*, 29/3 (1990), 297–314.

—— "Why Strict Churches are Strong," *American Journal of Sociology*, 99 (1994), 1180–1211.

IKEDA, DAISAKU, "Take Responsibility for your Life," Speech to the 1st Okinawa Executive Conference, Onnason, Japan, Feb. 23 1997; repr. in *World Tribune* (Apr. 18 1997), 9, 11.

INGLEHART, RONALD, *Culture Shift in Advanced Industrial Society* (Princeton: Princeton University Press, 1988).

JACOBS, JANET, *Divine Disenchantment* (Bloomington: Indiana University Press, 1989).

JOHNSON, ALLAN, *Statistics* (San Diego: Harcourt, Brace, Jovanovich, 1988).

JORDAN, BILL, *The Common Good: Citizenship, Morality, and Self-Interest* (New York: Basil Blackwell, 1987).

MACHACEK, DAVID, "Generation X and Religion: The General Social Survey Data," Paper presented at the Annual Meeting of the Society for the Scientific Study of Religion, Nashville, Tenn., 1996.

MARTY, MARTIN, *Modern American Religion*, i: *The Irony of it All, 1893–1919* (Chicago: University of Chicago Press, 1986).

—— *Modern American Religion*, ii: *The Noise of Conflict, 1919–1941* (Chicago: University of Chicago Press, 1991).

MAUSS, ARMAND L, "Dimensions of Defection," *Review of Religious Research*, 10 (1969), 128–35.

MELTON, J. GORDON, *Encyclopedia of American Religions*, 4th edn. (Detroit: Gale Research Inc., 1993).

METRAUX, DANIEL, "The Dispute between the Soka Gakkai and the Nichiren Shoshu Priesthood: A Lay Revolution against a Conservative Clergy," *Japanese Journal of Religious Studies*, 19/4 (1992), 325–36.

—— *The History and Theology of Soka Gakkai: A Japanese New Religion* (Lewiston, NY: Edwin Mellen, 1988).

MEYER, JOHN, and ROWAN, BRIAN, "Institutionalized Organizations: Formal Structure as Myth and Ceremony," in Walter Powell and Paul DiMaggio (eds.), *The New Institutionalism in Organizational Analysis* (Chicago: University of Chicago Press, 1991).

NAKANO, TSUYOSHI, "New Religions and Politics in Post-War Japan," *Sociologica*, 14/12 (1990),

NEEDLEMAN, JACOB, *The New Religions* (Garden City, NY: Doubleday, 1970).

NSA Quarterly (Summer 1976).

RAY, PAUL, "The Emerging Culture," *American Demographics*, 19/2 (1997), 29–34, 56.

RICHARDSON, JAMES T., *Conversion Careers: In and Out of the New Religions* (Beverly Hills, Calif.: Sage, 1977).

ROBBINS, THOMAS, *Cults, Converts and Charisma* (London: Sage, 1988).

ROOF, Wade Clark, *A Generation of Seekers: The Spiritual Journeys of the Baby Boom Generation.* (San Francisco: Harper San Francisco, 1993).

—— and McKINNEY, WILLIAM, *American Mainline Religion: Its Changing Shape and Future* (New Brunswick, NJ: Rutgers University Press, 1987).

SKONOVD, NORMAN, "Apostasy: The Process of Defection from Religious Totalism," Ph.D. thesis, Ann Arbor, Mich.: University Microfilms International, 1981.

SLATER, DON, *Consumer Culture and Modernity* (Cambridge, Mass.: Basil Blackwell, 1997).

SNOW, DAVID, *Shakubuku: A Study of the Nichiren Shoshu Buddhist Movement in America, 1960–75* (New York: Garland, 1993).

"Soka Gakkai's Relations with the Komei Party," *Soka Gakkai News* (Sept. 1994), 20–1.

STARK, RODNEY, and BAINBRIDGE, WILLIAM SIMS, *The Future of Religion: Secularization, Revival, and Cult Formation* (Berkeley: University of California Press, 1985).

STONE, JACQUELINE, "Rebuking the Enemies of the Lotus: Nichirenist Exclusivism in Historical Perspective," *Japanese Journal of Religious Studies*, 21/2–3 (1994), 231–59.

TIPTON, STEVEN, *Getting Saved from the Sixties* (Berkeley: University of California Press, 1982).

TOCQUEVILLE, ALEXIS DE, *Democracy in America*, trans. G. Lawrence (Garden City, NY: Anchor Books, 1969).

US Department of Justice, Immigration and Naturalization Service, *Annual Reports of the Immigration and Naturalization Service* (Washington: Government Printing Office, 1966–1976).

—— *Statistical Yearbooks of the Immigration and Naturalization Service* ([1980?]–1994).

WEBER, MAX, *The Protestant Ethic and the Spirit of Capitalism*, trans. Talcott Parsons (Los Angeles: Roxbury, 1998).

—— *The Theory of Social and Economic Organization*, trans. Talcott Parsons (New York: Free Press, 1947).

WHITE, JAMES, *The Soka Gakkai and Mass Society* (Stanford, Calif.: Stanford University Press, 1970).

WILLIAMS, GEORGE M., *Freedom and Influence: The Role of Religion in American Society (An NSA Perspective)* (Santa Monica, Calif.: World Tribune Press, 1985).

—— *NSA Seminar Report 1968–71* (Santa Monica, Calif.: World Tribune Press, 1972).

WILSON, BRYAN, and DOBBELAERE, KAREL, *A Time to Chant: The Soka Gakkai Buddhists in Britain* (Oxford: Clarendon Press, 1994).

WRIGHT, STUART A., *Leaving Cults: The Dynamics of Defection* (Washington: Society for the Scientific Study of Religion, 1987).

Glossary

daimoku   see *Nam-myoho-renge-kyo*

Gohonzon   the sacred scroll inscribed by Nichiren, and the object of worship

gongyo   recital of two chapters of the *Lotus Sutra*, a ritual undertaken morning and evening

Gosho   the collected writings of Nichiren

hokkeko   lay organizations associated with the temples

Komeito   literally "clean government party"

kosen-rufu   the spread of Buddhism in the world

mappo   the latter day of the law (namely, the present age)

Nam-myoho-renge-kyo   the invocation of the *Lotus Sutra*

shakubuku   literally "break and subdue" (false teachings)—the vigorous method of proselytizing

shoju   the "show by example" approach to recruitment

Soka Gakkai   Value Creation Society

toba   memorial tablets offered on behalf of the dead

zui ho bini   the adaptation of the precept to the locality (justifying the acceptance of local cultural conditions)

Index